STOP TOLERANCE

A GUIDE TO ZERO TOLERANCE AND REGAIN YOURSELF TO LIVE YOUR BEST LIFE

Manikanta Belde

Contents

Why I wrote this book?

Tolerance in life has caused me great suffering. I listened to other people's advice and gave up on my own desires. I followed instructions from others frequently. I too, like many others, have been told many lies about success. I chose a different career, and it caused me to suffer. I decided to embrace a new way of life, convinced that aiming for big dreams was out of reach for me. However, this choice brought about frustration and remorse in my existence. Nevertheless, these experiences have served as a powerful muse, igniting within me the motivation to write this book.

I have made the decision to assist individuals who, like myself, aspire to turn their dreams into reality. My objective is to guide people towards the understanding of truth, rather than allowing them to be trapped in false beliefs. I want to witness people transform and improve themselves. I have developed a concept called "stop tolerance," which emphasizes that we only receive what we are willing to accept in life." Hence, we must never settle for anything that falls short of our rightful entitlement. We deserve better and we are more capable.

Allow me to clarify this concept using an illustration.

<u>ILLUSTRATION FOR STOP TOLERANCE CONCEPT</u>

but with weights
attached to your feet
Can you fly easily or
will the weights drag
you down?

No ,right? You cannot
fly and will be pulled
back to the ground.

What if you were asked to soar in the sky using a parachute, but with weights attached to your feet? These weights are twice as heavy as you.

Could you still glide effortlessly and reach great heights? The answer is no.

This scenario mirrors our lives. We all aspire for greatness, longing to rise high in life's journey. However, we're often held back by self-imposed burdens pulling us down.

These burdens could be family pressures, societal expectations, poor mindset or inferiority complex among others. They limit our ascension towards success and personal growth.

To truly ascend and achieve your goals, it's crucial to free yourself from these ties that bind us down. Only when these shackles are shed can we grow personally and lead a meaningful life of impact.

You must stop tolerating the burdens that weigh us down and restrict our ability to soar.

Who is this book for?

Do you keep tolerating things in life? Do you often find yourself feeling restless when you have to go through something? Do you have trouble succeeding in different aspects of life such as business, relationships, career, and self-discipline?

If so, you might need - Stop Tolerance.

In today's world, where people use people and people love things, tolerance became a barrier to success and happiness. We are constantly being used by people every day for their needs. If you constantly deal with toxic situations and people, it can hold you back from succeeding in life. Most people ignore this simple thing and suffer life more than living it to the fullest.

These toxic people and situations become lifetime addictions that prevent our growth, and this is a painful truth you need to realize now. We often settle for comfort and familiarity instead of pursuing our dreams. It is common for us to let outside influences shape our behavior and limit our actions. This ultimately results in us settling for our current situation instead of taking charge and striving for what we really want. It's important to recognize these influences and take ownership of our lives.

If we keep accepting things that are bad for us, we are no longer in control of our own lives. We become puppets, letting others control us indefinitely. We become restless, anxious, frustrated, and mentally weak when we live someone else's life by tolerating their rules and ideas.

But it doesn't have to be this way.

When you learn to stop tolerating things and people that limit you, you grow into a better version of yourself. You achieve more. You become self-disciplined. You become better at choosing your career or running your business. You become better at finding and managing relationships better, and ultimately you will live a life that matters to you the most.

Are you ready to let go of things and people in your life and reclaim your life back to you and live it to the fullest?

More specifically, in this Stop Tolerance book, you will learn to:

Stop tolerating people who are harmful to you.

Stop accepting whatever comes to you.

Becoming mentally strong and disciplined.

Becoming wild from being tamed by society.

Take more risks and see life from a different perspective.

Becoming better at career, business, and relationships.

If the above topics interest you, read on.

Introduction

Tell me if this is you:

You know that if you could stop tolerating toxicity and inferiority in life, you could bring in more joy and wisdom into life. You know very well that a career you love will make you joyful. Your business idea makes you feel good. Your right relationships will make you feel great. You achieve your desires and make your life purposeful by living the way you love.

But you never seem to realize this.

Instead of focusing on yourself and your desires first, you end up accepting the false beliefs and ideas of the world. You tolerate what you should not tolerate, and you don't tolerate what you should tolerate. You may settle for a career that doesn't offer you the pay you truly deserve, despite your qualifications and hard work. It's time to start pushing for higher compensation and seek out opportunities that value your skills and experience. You deserve to succeed and thrive in a career that reflects your true worth.

You tolerate and accept toxic people in life because you are scared of loneliness. You accept and tolerate your position right now because that is what people around you taught you. You tolerate no respect in different situations from people because you are scared of people. This list goes on and on in different instances of life.

Have you been in any situations mentioned above?

If so, you will greatly benefit from this book. We'll show you simple ways, examples, and narratives to help you stop being too accommodating and become skilled in living without compromising for others. You'll also learn to handle any situation life throws your way.

So, are you up for the challenge?

In Part 1, Stop Tolerance concept and the role it plays, we will explain what the idea is and how it works. By reading this section, you'll learn why breaking the habit of tolerating things in different areas of your life is crucial. You'll also understand how tolerating everything can negatively impact your personal development and happiness.

In part 2, The Problem, we will see why tolerance is bad for us. Here we'll talk about analogies and stories that help us grasp the importance of ditching the habit of tolerance for good.

In part 3, the benefits of the stop tolerance concept, we will review all the reasons and benefits of the stop tolerance concept. We will introduce a number of different types of methods to practice stop tolerance concepts in everyday life.

In part 4, A 7-step method for zero tolerance, we will cover a 7-step approach for zero tolerance. This section will provide detailed instructions on how to effectively incorporate the stop tolerance concept into your work environment. The seven steps outlined will be straightforward and easy to follow, ensuring successful implementation for all.

In part 5, doing the work (and overcoming tolerance), we will discuss how this concept of stop tolerance can be implemented in everyday life. You will learn to make this concept a go-to rule for life to see the true side of life.

In Part 6, which is all about avoiding tolerance relapse, offers some straightforward tools and techniques that will assist you in preventing yourself from falling back into old habits. By implementing these strategies, you will be able to stay on track for an extended period of time until maintaining your new habits becomes second nature to you.

PART 1
Stop Tolerance Concept and the Role it Plays

You have probably heard from people that tolerance is very important in life. You must tolerate things in life. Toleration makes you strong. These sayings are true only for a few things. But we started implementing this to everything in life, which made us fail to understand it.

Tolerating what helps us grow is fine, but tolerating what breaks us down is not fine, and it's foolishness. The sad part is most people are still dwelling in such foolishness, believing that tolerating is good, which is a lie.

It's good to endure stress and pain while working towards something you want, but it's not good to endure stress for something you hate. Tolerating people who make you happy is good but tolerating people who break you is bad. Tolerating a job that you love is good but tolerating a job you hate is bad even though it pays well.

Tolerating criticism from people you love is good but tolerating criticism from people you hate or don't know is bad. Tolerance is a wide concept that applies to every part of life. Understanding when to tolerate and when not to tolerate is what separates you from being happy or sad.

Stop tolerance concept is not a complex concept. It's a simple concept that teaches you just one particular thing. We get what we tolerate in life. So tolerate what is important for our growth and happiness and get rid of something that is not helping you grow or limiting your growth.

This concept applies to most areas in life. Take from some basic areas such as self-discipline to how we allow people to treat us, relationships, careers and the way we live our whole lives.

You need to understand that you can't have happiness and growth along wrong tolerance. As people are always confused about what is right or wrong tolerance or as they are getting manipulated as they both are the same. It's important to stop tolerating in life as much as possible.

By doing so you allow yourself to come out of the people's spell of controlling us and this enables us to be free and live a life that matters to us.

To sum up, stop tolerance concept helps you understand that tolerance is bad at most parts of life so its good thing to get rid of tolerance. Unfortunately, it's not easy to break this as we are all hardwired to believe that tolerance is important in life but the fast is quite the opposite.

When you understand that being too tolerant can hinder your personal growth and happiness, you'll recognize what has held you back from wellness and progress.

Action Step:

Using your action guide, answer these questions.

What are the 3 things that you tolerate every day?

Is tolerating these things giving you happiness?

If not, why are you tolerating them?

If the reasons are not in your favor, how can you break them?

Wisdom Snippet #1

"True transformation begins when we refuse to tolerate our own limitations and instead push ourselves beyond what we thought possible."

PART 2
The problem

We have previously seen the positive impact of strict adherence to zero tolerance on our personal growth. This section will uncover why tolerance is bad for growth and how to shield yourself from the tolerance pitfalls that are present in our society.

The tolerance at everything.

People constantly remind you that you must be tolerant if you want to succeed in life. It's partially true, but there's more to it. Accepting certain things is acceptable, especially if it doesn't harm your growth or happiness. But to accept everything with no thought is not a good approach.

Society attempts to keep us under its control through the expectation that we should tolerate and compromise. You heard correctly. We are all born wild, but society tames us to fit in it. Most people are settling for less in their lives without considering the effects. They accept negative situations - a bad job, a bad relationship, a dishonest government, no recognition, a bad lifestyle, and lies.

Limitations prevent us from growing and living life to the fullest. Therefore, tolerating them is counterproductive. Becoming conscious of our limitations and taking action empowers us to lead a boundless life, fulfilling our highest potential. Tolerance extends beyond specific circumstances and applies to a wide range of experiences in our lives. This includes:

- A bad career choice

- A toxic relationship you chose because of fear of loneliness

- Accepting criticism from people

- Lies they taught you, and you believe strongly

- No respect

- Wrong Judgment

- No Discipline

- This list goes on.

Is there anything on this list or beyond that you find yourself putting up with? Does tolerating any of it bring you joy? The majority of answers would likely be negative. If you are unable to engage in activities that foster personal development, you may be tolerating a situation that is unsuitable for you. Identifying the hindrances that restrict your growth and taking action against them can remarkably enhance your life.

Action Step

Using your workbook, write down a past situation when you didn't tolerate something that made you happy. Are there any situations that made you really happy and feel proud of yourself? List them here.

Your dreams are being taken over without your consent.

The things that you choose to tolerate hold significant importance. What may come as a surprise is that what you accept is what you ultimately receive. People in power teach false beliefs and rules in the name of good to control you and make you tolerate things that limit you. In the process, you lose your beautiful dreams. Many of these beliefs you learn are made to work at the subconscious level, which makes it very hard to break them and pursue your dreams.

Let me give you an example at career level. Remember what people around you taught you about your career? Did they tell you to dream big? Did they teach you to take the most risk? Did they allow you to become what you love? Did they tell you to choose any career other than engineering or doctor? (or anything you love pursuing). For most people, for most questions the answer is very simple: it's a NO.

If it's not your case, you are very lucky.

The sad part is you agreed to what they taught you and what they allowed. In simple terms, you tolerated what they said blindly. Does this tolerance make you happy? I feel that career is something we are going to spend a lot of time with. If it's something you hate, imagine what kind of life you are going to live. It feels scary to live in hell. Isn't it?

Waking up to something you don't like or love and spending all your time in it without any interest is not life at all. It's purely wasting your life. Life is shorter than you think. If you keep tolerating wrong against important aspects of life, you are going to waste your life for sure.

People often tolerate jobs they dislike due to family, social or financial pressures, or societal expectations. Do you think it's fair to do so? I say NO. There is always a way to break this tolerance and choose a career you love. How to do it may not be clear now but if you keep trying to find ways you will surely come up with a solution.

You may come across news of people who achieved their desires irrespective of the troubles they are in just like you. What makes them stand out is they don't agree or tolerate or compromise because of their situation. Instead, they find ways to get what they want irrespective of the risks they have to take. When you change your perception of tolerance and compromise, you will also be able to achieve more in life and pursue your career. Below are some ways to prevent career tolerance:

- **Don't believe blindly what people say**. Carefully consider before accepting career guidance from others. It's important to verify if people are speaking based on their knowledge or just making assumptions or drawing from their personal experiences. Getting advice from people who have had similar experiences is very helpful because they have real-life knowledge that they can share effectively.

- **Research well and don't be in a hurry.** Take as much time as you need to explore your passions and meticulously research the career path you wish to pursue. Try to imagine the long-term impact that it would have on your emotions and quality of life. If pursuing that brings you joy, then, by all means, pursue it.

- **Stop saying excuses**. People often have reasons for not pursuing things in their lives. Making excuses prevents experiencing joy and greatness while taking responsibility and overcoming obstacles leads to fulfillment and happiness. Now it's your turn to make a choice.

- **Be disciplined and start now**. The truth is that in most cases, there is no "right time" and waiting for it is just a myth that many people choose to believe. The concept of the "right time" is nonexistent. Begin working toward your passion without delay once you've discovered it. Develop a well-structured strategy, establish a daily routine, and strive to make gradual progress each day.

Action step

Use the workbook and write 5 goals you have when you were a child. List them according to your priority. Now write reasons you want to pursue them. Are there dreams your own or someone told you about them? Have you achieved those dreams? If Yes, are you happy? If No, why didn't you pursue them?

Your relationship may be a lie.

Our careers are important, but we must not forget the significant impact relationships have on our lives. Our job affects our happiness and our relationships affect our mental health. Having strong bonds with others is essential to lead a fulfilling life. It's important to be aware that the majority of relationships are built on deceit in today's world. They might be present either for their own benefit or out of fear of loneliness. Let me make it clear to you.

Imagine if a relative who you strongly despise showed up at your doorstep. Everyone at home makes the relative feel comfortable. You are uncomfortable. You treat them well because that relative won't be there permanently. Have you considered the potential consequences of being involved in a relationship or friendship with someone who doesn't positively impact your personal development? Staying with someone due to addiction may hinder your personal growth; however, leaving them can be a difficult decision. Do you think the relationship is making you happy? No.

If someone is holding you back and keeping you from being the best you can be, the relationship is unhealthy and needs to be dealt with. Staying with an addicted person who doesn't want to improve is not honest and hinders your personal development. I believe that some of the relationships we create are actually built on falsehoods and therefore, cannot be considered genuine.

Staying in relationships that hinder your personal growth and happiness can be detrimental to your well-being. It is important to recognize when a relationship is no longer serving you and take steps to address the situation. By doing so, you can create space for healthier, more fulfilling relationships and experiences. You need to take care of them some way or else you will end up suffering a lot. You need to stop tolerating toxic relationships or friendships. Below are some ways to find and fix such relationships:

- **Communicate openly.** You need to talk openly about what you want and what they want. Share your expectations clearly. When you or they can't meet them, find alternatives or give up such relationship which turns you mad.

- **Love alone is not enough**. Love is said to be sufficient for any relationship. But that's a lie. In addition to love, a relationship requires commitment to each other, giving attention to your partner and being responsible for your actions. Being in a relationship means that you are willing to give everything that you can to your partner without holding back. If being in a relationship is not enjoyable or fulfilling, then it is probably best to avoid having one.

- **Accept and change**. If you come across imperfections that shake your relationship, try to embrace them and let go if changing them is not possible. If you have the ability to correct those imperfections, make the necessary changes. By fostering mutual understanding and growth, you contribute greatly to establishing a thriving relationship, an essential element for any healthy connection.

End the toxic relationship if nothing works. Don't keep tolerating them. They affect you greatly.

Action step

In the workbook, write the qualities that you hate in your partner and ask your partner to do the same. Once you find these flaws, mark them as CAN FIX and CAN'T FIX. Now write down your ideas or ways to fix them. Then share your ideas with each other.

Remember you deserve better.

We put up with things that are not necessary or suitable because we believe we don't deserve anything better. Isn't it true? Think about it.

We often accept things that are below our worth, which is why we continue to settle for less than we deserve. Accepting the belief that you don't deserve anything big may lead to a lower paying job, less respect and attention and increased self-doubt. This affects your happiness and mental health in the long term. This makes you settle for less and tolerate things that bring you down.

Changing our self-belief changes how we see things and helps us let go of negative experiences. You should always remember that you are worthy, and you have something unique and most importantly you are very important, and you deserve always better.

Action step

In the workbook, describe what you feel about yourself. All your positives and negatives. Now find whether those self-believes are true or not. If true and need some changes, find ways to fix them. Once you change your beliefs and become mentally strong, you start looking at life differently.

Wisdom Snippet #2

"Tolerate the things that are essential for growth and do not tolerate the things that are not necessary for growth."

PART 3
The benefits of Stop Tolerance

Ways to prevent intolerance and their benefits.

We have seen how tolerance habits affect various aspects of life. Our perception of ourselves, which may have been taught to us by others or developed on our own, is often the main cause of this habit. Breaking self-belief or perception is not so easy. It's a slow and long term process. But it's worthy. This is what stop tolerance is for.

What is Stop Tolerance?

The process called stop tolerance can be described as follows:

Learning to let go of tolerance towards things that hinder personal development in life. It's a way to handle life situations without compromising.

An important Note:

The term "Stop Tolerance" may not be the most accurate expression. Instead, I should be using "Zero Tolerance." However, I prefer to use "Stop Tolerance" as a mantra in any situation where you are about to endure something detrimental to you. The concept of STOP TOLERANCE is a crucial one to keep in mind.

Stop tolerance helps you in making right decisions that help you in personal growth, relationships, career and so on. This guide is a winding journey that leads you back to rediscover yourself after facing countless obstacles in this world.

Now let's have a look at what you will learn from this book. In this book, I will introduce you to different types of tolerance and the ways to deal with them effectively.

- The 7-week complete stop tolerance plan

- The 7-day stop tolerance plan

- The 7-hour stop tolerance plan

Let's talk more about each process and how they work.

The 7-week complete stop tolerance plan

This is the most efficient and rigorous stop tolerance strategy. The idea is very easy to understand. With this method, it's possible to address multiple habits all at once.

You must eliminate tolerance from your day-to-day life for 7 weeks completely. Consider every small situation in your life. Don't compromise or tolerate anything. Dong so can assist you in breaking free from the patterns of tolerance that have become deeply ingrained in you over time. You will be much better, and you will understand what is true and what is not. You'll understand situations better and see people's genuine nature in some cases.

By eliminating all kinds of tolerance, I mean you need to eliminate all the following daily to daily tolerances for 7 weeks completely:

- criticism from others

- judgment of others about you

- laziness

- indiscipline

- toxic friends

- toxic relationships

- fake people

- fake beliefs

- lies from others

- bad career

- less pay

- less respect

- and so on.

Each of the above are regular examples in life. Stop tolerating them.

You might be asking, won't it be rude?

I would say, it's alright and here are some suggestions to make this plan work well:

- Inform people around you that you are up for a challenge of zero tolerance.

- Meditate every day to stay calm

- Always chant Stop Tolerance when you get into a situation where you have to tolerate something.

- If you forgot about the plan, don't worry. It's alright. Try not repeating it many times.

- Don't divide and judge what is good and what is bad while preventing tolerance.

- Always remember that this is a game for 7 weeks to improve yourself.

- Record your experiences every day and reflect on them. (Observe how you feel)

After finishing the 7-week program, take some time to reflect on your emotions and ideas. It is beneficial to distinguish between tolerances that benefit and harm you. Choose the favorable ones and maintain the momentum of your progress by adhering to your current stop tolerance routine each day.

The 7-day stop tolerance plan

It's like a shorter version of the 7-week plan. Not very effective since zero tolerance is only enforced for a week. Trying this approach may not guarantee a lasting change, as you may fall back into your old patterns. However, testing it out could prompt you to devise a strategy for decreasing your tolerance over time. This type of plan is also useful for working out a few tolerance habits at once.

The 7-hour stop tolerance plan

The effectiveness of this plan is limited when used only once, due to its brevity. If you use it often, it works very well. It is particularly helpful when focusing on a single negative tolerance behavior. If you want to work on one tolerance behavior at a time, I would recommend this 7-hour plan. This plan could work as a trial to combat tolerance. You only need 7 hours of your day to try out this plan. To truly comprehend the effectiveness of the 7-hour stop tolerance challenge, make a conscious effort to stay active throughout the entire duration of the challenge.

IMPORTANT NOTE:

I want you to remember that: be right through the journey while executing any of the above plans. Not good nor kind. Just BE RIGHT. This is because when you are good and kind, you will be manipulated by your mind to tolerate certain things again, which makes you fail the challenge.

Action plan

In the workbook, write your experiences (results) for any kind of plan you followed. After every experience, share your feelings as good, bad or moderate. This helps you understand the effectiveness of the plan.

Wisdom Snippet #3

"In the absence of tolerance, we discover our resilience, adaptability, and ultimately, our ability to rise above any obstacle."

PART 4
A 7-step method for zero tolerance

This section will present you with a straightforward 7-step approach focused on zero tolerance that will aid you to rediscover yourself and live limitlessly.

Step #1. Clarify Your Values and Vision

This is the first important step before we proceed forward. Define your goals and values before pursuing success. Think about your fundamental values and goals for your future.

Now take a sheet of paper and a pen. Now write What do you want to achieve in life? What are your limits right now? What is holding you back? What can be done to achieve what you want without compromising. (You can use the space in the workbook if needed)

Now, once you answer the above questions. Write the list of what are you tolerating that is preventing you from reaching your goal.

Expand on your ideas as much as you want. Don't limit yourself. Now, once you finish the list, write your ideas or ways to prevent tolerance. Keep this list aside, and it works as a rough plan to overcome tolerance barriers for you.

Situation:

Mr. Arjun wants to pursue his career as a sportsman, but he could not afford a sports school. His parents and family told him to quit his goal and look for some job that pays well.

Now do you think Arjun should give up on his goal and go for a job? Or do you think Arjun has to find a way to fulfill his dream? Or do you have any other solution?

Arjun is determined to pursue his dream of becoming a successful athlete. His problem is money. If he tolerates his economic situation, he can't achieve his goal.

Now we know his goal and problem. Accepting the situation and compromising makes him lose his goal. Now he has to find his way to pursue his goal.

List could be:

- He will work hard and keep trying.

- He will ask for help.

- He will keep practicing and try to prove himself by taking every small or big opportunity.

- He should take up the job and also work on his dream in his free time.

- And there could be more solutions or ways or ideas.

The more he thinks, the more ways he produces. Believing that his economic condition bars him from achieving anything will prevent him from reaching his goals.

Numerous athletes have risen from poverty and surmounted multiple obstacles to achieve great success. Every day, many artists, entrepreneurs, visionaries, and not only sportsmen, serve as a source of inspiration to us. They have demonstrated that merely enduring our limitations will not lead to success in life; rather, surpassing them is the key. They are the living proof.

Step #2. Identify Non-Negotiable Behaviors

Identify behaviors that are non-negotiable towards your goals that make up your zero-tolerance list. Make sure that these align with your core values.

List all the behaviors that should not be tolerated to achieve the goal. We cannot tolerate such behavior under any circumstances. In order to overcome old limiting beliefs and ineffective behaviors, a complete redesign of your internal environment is necessary. This approach assists you in devising a strategy to accomplish great objectives efficiently.

Situation:

As we know Mr. Arjun already, let's continue building the plan for him.

Our paperwork has been completed, and now we must identify all the behaviors that are non-negotiable. In order to achieve your goal, it's crucial to avoid these behaviors in any circumstance. What behaviors do you think will limit Mr. Arjun?

The list may look like this:

- Self-doubt

- Lack of confidence

- Inferiority

- Blind belief in people who told Arjun to pursue a job

- Accepting societal rules

- and so on.

All the behaviors in the list are non-negotiable and should not be tolerated by us. Our second step is complete with this.

Step #3. Communicate Clearly

Communicate your expectations clearly with others and let them know about the behaviors that are not acceptable to you. Use assertive communication techniques.

Oftentimes, the biggest obstacle lies within ourselves. An additional issue we face is the influence of the individuals in our surroundings. To make this approach work well, we need discipline and support from others to minimize disruptions and maximize efficiency.

Situation:

Arjun now has a clear goal and has identified his problematic behaviors which cannot be ignored. He needs to communicate before executing his plan. He needs to share his plan with those around him positively, explaining what he wants to achieve and how they can support him.

In order to successfully accomplish his goals, it is essential that he sets clear rules for those in his vicinity to minimize interruptions.

Arjun may share the following rules:

- Avoid giving him advice to go for a job.

- Give him some amount of time to prove himself.

- Help him someway to meet people

- Let him know about any sports happening around.

- Not to criticize or laugh at him.

- Not to judge him.

- And so on.

Once everything is ready, the plan can be executed well.

Step #4. Set Limits

Establish clear limits with yourself and others regarding behavior, attitude, or situations that contradict your zero-tolerance list.

We have already made pre-arrangements. Now it's time to set limits. Limits that are useful for growth. Set limits for yourself in terms of time, habits and false beliefs. This helps you work on your plan effectively.

This step can contain the following:

- Time limit in which you will achieve your goal

- Your attitude towards your goals. Make sure it's always positive

- A disciplined plan or schedule which breaks your plan into parts

- Limiting your false beliefs you learned and people taught

Situation:

Arjun must conquer his mental obstacles by challenging his limiting beliefs. Maintaining a positive attitude is crucial for him at all times. He should refuse to accept anything that hinders his progress toward achieving his objective. He can set different limits for listing and restricting. Even you may have different barriers which should not be tolerated.

Step #5. Hold Yourself Accountable

Be accountable in following through on the promises you make to yourself and others regarding the limits set around unacceptable behaviors and actions.

Although having a great plan is a good start, it does not guarantee great results in every situation. Greatness requires one to overcome hardships. Making mistakes is a natural part of being human, as we all have imperfections. We must take responsibility for any problems that arise while promoting intolerance of harmful or discriminatory behaviors. Instead of assigning blame to someone or a particular circumstance, it would be more productive to focus on finding solutions to the problem at hand. Instead of playing the blame game, we should focus on rectifying our mistakes and continue moving forward with our plan.

Situation:

By eradicating all sorts of tolerance and setting limits for himself as well as for others, Arjun effectively executed his plan. This is likely to cause problems. He shouldn't quit. He should remain positive and take responsibility for all outcomes. This contributes to his mental fortitude and empowers him to push forward.

Step #6. Focus On Solutions Over Problems

In case of setbacks or obstacles, adopt a solution-oriented approach over negativity or counterproductive thinking habits.

Problems happen in every process. A sense of negativity emerges. Although mistakes can hinder progress, they are valuable learning opportunities that can drive us to seek solutions and achieve success. As you strive to abstain from tolerance, obstacles are bound to surface. Perhaps the issue stems from either the circumstances or an individual. If you worry about it and quit, growth won't happen. So, just focus on solutions and growth and ignore everything else.

Situation:

Arjun could have several problems. He could make enemies while working towards his goal. He could lose support as he's too focused on his goal. Without money, he could go hungry for a period of time. Success is the outcome of overcoming every problem or obstacle that emerges in your path, despite the uncertainty of the outcome.

Step #7. Empower Yourself With Boundaries

Don't be afraid of missing out on social connections or opportunities that involve behaviors you don't tolerate. Instead, see it as a way to feel in control.

When you quit tolerating, you'll inevitably need to give up certain things. Some people will inevitably slip away from you. Failure to maintain your connections could result in their loss. If you continue this behavior, it's likely that you'll end up pushing away the people you care about. Don't worry, success will come to you eventually. And if you happen to fail, take it as an opportunity to learn from people and situations in order to grow personally.

Seize this moment to be self-disciplined, cherish every minute, don't get too comfortable, and enjoy life completely.

Situation:

Arjun's determination and perseverance through numerous obstacles will undoubtedly lead him to triumph and grant him liberation from many tolerances in the near future.

Embracing a zero-tolerance attitude doesn't mean being narrow-minded. It signifies respecting yourself, fostering positive relationships in your personal and professional life, and striving towards fulfilling your life's mission by continuously improving.

Although at first glance it may seem like a mere strategy to achieve a goal, upon closer examination, it becomes clear that this plan entails cultivating an unwavering intolerance towards your own behavior, habits, the people around you, and difficult situations.

Tips to make the most out of this plan

Here are some tips to help you make the most of this plan and increase its effectiveness:

Write your experiences every day.

Keep a daily journal where you record everything that happens throughout your day. Share your thoughts, experiences, and situations that caused anxiety. Share your knowledge, your mistakes, and all the crucial details. It becomes systematic record of the plan for – stop tolerance idea.

Reflect on these thoughts

Focusing solely on making progress can cause you to overlook important aspects. Taking some time to reflect on your thoughts will improve your understanding of the situation.

- **Reflect on your limits:** Discover what has been constraining you for such a prolonged period of time. Is the circumstance at fault, or perhaps a single person, or possibly your own misconceptions? Once you identify the barriers that are holding you back, rectifying them becomes a simple task.

- **Evaluate how you spend your time:** Discover how you are allocating your time constraints. Are you truly maximizing your time or allowing it to slip away unused? If you have tasks that don't help your plan, solve the problem and organize the time for each task again.

- **Break your fear:** The main obstacle to achieving growth is fear. It hinders our abilities and makes us accept unpleasant things regularly. This fear is the reason why many individuals do not succeed in their personal growth. Fear is the reason that prevents us from taking action. Instead of letting fear hold you back, I recommend setting it aside as an illusion while working on your plan. This will allow you to take necessary risks and achieve highly effective results.

- **Break your beliefs for a while:** Everyone has beliefs. Some things are true and some are false. Focus on your personal growth instead of being tied to any specific belief system.

- **Be selfish for a while:** Although it is often considered negative, being self-centered can have various consequences, depending on the situation. I have some important information to share with you. Prioritize your personal growth, even if it means being self-centered. It is acceptable to prioritize your own interests, as long as your actions do not negatively impact others.

Wisdom Snippet #4

"Tolerance may breed comfort, but embracing discomfort breeds personal growth that knows no limits."

PART 5
Overcoming every type of tolerance

Stop tolerance guide aims to help you develop beneficial tolerance habits. It's important to learn to tolerate, but it's also important to unlearn certain types of tolerance. In this part, we will discuss different types of tolerance that you should unlearn. Developing a few tolerant habits focused on personal development and self-improvement can be highly beneficial and necessary. It's crucial to eliminate any tolerance that hinders your personal growth as soon as possible.

The types of tolerance we should develop include:

1. **Cultural Tolerance:** It is important to acknowledge and appreciate the diversity of cultures, traditions and beliefs around us. By embracing these differences, we can gain a greater understanding and perspective of the world and the people in it. It is also essential to show respect for others' beliefs, even if they differ from our own. This creates a harmonious and inclusive society where everyone feels valued and accepted.

2. **Open-mindedness:** Keep an open mind to unfamiliar concepts and viewpoints, regardless of their contrast to yours.

3. **Patience:** It is important to remain patient, especially in difficult circumstances. Doing so will enable you to gain a better perspective and make more informed choices.

4. **Emotional Tolerance**: It is important to become skilled at handling and controlling your emotions, as well as comprehending and sympathizing with the feelings of others.

5. **Ambiguity Tolerance:** Acquiring skills to manage uncertainty and ambiguity is crucial because we often face situations where there is no straightforward answer. Life is full of unclear situations, and it is important to learn how to handle them appropriately. Sometimes we have to make decisions without all the necessary information. In those cases, having the ability to cope with ambiguity can be incredibly valuable.

6. **Diversity Tolerance:** It is important to appreciate and acknowledge diversity in various forms, such as race, ethnicity, gender, sexual orientation, and abilities. Celebrating different perspectives and backgrounds can lead to a more inclusive and supportive environment for all. By recognizing and valuing diversity, we can create a better and more equitable society for everyone.

7. **Intellectual Tolerance:** It is important to participate in conversations and arguments with consideration for others' intellectual beliefs and be receptive to new ideas.

8. **Generosity:** To develop tolerance towards others, it is important to exhibit acts of kindness, compassion and generosity. By doing so, we can create an environment that fosters respect and empathy towards others regardless of their dif-

ferences.

9. **Forgiveness**: One important thing that you can do for your personal growth and healing is to practice forgiveness and let go of grudges. Holding onto past hurt can weigh you down and prevent you from moving forward in life. By cultivating forgiveness, you can release any negative energy and make space for positivity and healing.

10. **Flexibility:** It's important to stay flexible and willing to make changes to your plans and expectations as circumstances change. By adapting to new situations, you'll be better equipped to navigate unexpected challenges and achieve your goals.

11. **Resilience:** It's important to develop resilience in order to cope with setbacks and challenges, and to have the determination to persist through tough times. By building resilience, individuals can increase their ability to bounce back from difficult situations. This can involve developing coping strategies, practicing self-care, and seeking support when needed. Ultimately, resilience can help individuals to thrive in the face of adversity.

12. **Self-acceptance:** One of the most important things in life is to learn to accept ourselves just the way we are. This means acknowledging both our positive traits and our flaws. Developing a healthy and realistic self-image can foster more meaningful and satisfying relationships with others. Ultimately, self-acceptance is the key to happiness and personal fulfillment.

13. **Intercultural Tolerance:** It is important to acknowledge and value diversity in our interactions with people from different cultures. This includes being respectful of their customs, traditions, and ways of communicating. By embracing diversity, we can create a more inclusive and understanding environment.

14. **Acceptance of Differences:** It's important to respect and embrace diversity among individuals, which may manifest through differences in their ideas, ideologies, and principles. We should cultivate an attitude of acceptance and avoid making assumptions or stereotypes about others based on these differences. A non-judgmental approach to individual differences can go a long way in creating a harmonious and peaceful environment for everyone.

15. **Constructive Criticism:** It's important to have a mindset of receiving and giving constructive criticism. Such feedback can help individuals improve and grow on a personal level.

All these types of tolerance have to be developed for personal growth. By carefully observing, one can notice that these standards are rooted in personal convictions, driving self-improvement, whereas other tolerances could hinder personal development. Now let's talk about all the forms of tolerance that you ought to abandon.

The type of tolerance we should stop developing:

1. **Tolerance for mediocrity:** If we settle for the minimum requirements in life, we may miss out on opportunities for greater happiness and success in our personal and professional lives. It's important to embrace challenges and strive

for growth, rather than settling for mediocrity. By pushing ourselves out of our comfort zones, we can unlock our true potential and create a sense of purpose and fulfillment in our lives.

2. **Tolerance for toxic relationships:** Staying in toxic romantic relationships can harm our ability to form positive connections and have negative effects on our mental and emotional health. It is important to recognize when a relationship is unhealthy and have the strength to let go, thereby opening ourselves up to more fulfilling connections.

3. **Tolerance for discrimination:** All types of discrimination should be condemned and eradicated since they promote inequality and threaten human dignity. Such discriminative actions include racism, sexism, homophobia, and various other types of discrimination. Treat everyone with respect and provide equal opportunities, no matter their race, gender or sexual orientation, for a fair and just society. Hence, discrimination, in any form, must never be tolerated.

4. **Tolerance for procrastination:** Procrastination can have harmful effects in both personal and professional aspects. It can result in wasted time, missed opportunities, and decreased productivity. Therefore, it is important to establish good habits and manage time effectively to avoid the negative impact of procrastination.

5. **Tolerance for ignorance:** Being closed-minded and not accepting information that contradicts our beliefs can impede our growth and development. It is important to be open to

new ideas and perspectives to continue advancing.

6. **Tolerance for verbal abuse/negativity:** When we engage in constant negative self-talk or speak badly about others, it can harm our mental health and damage our relationships with ourselves and others. Therefore, it's crucial to practice positive self-talk and speak kindly about others to promote a healthy and supportive mindset. This kind of behavior can harm our self-esteem and lead to mental distress.

7. **Tolerance of bad habits:** Allowing bad habits to continue will only make them harder to break and stop us from achieving personal growth. Whether it's putting things off, eating unhealthy foods, or engaging in harmful actions, these habits will become more ingrained the longer we permit them. We must take action and stop tolerating them if we want to improve ourselves and our lives.

8. **Tolerance of toxic people:** Surrounding ourselves with negative or toxic people can drain our energy and hinder our personal growth. Instead of tolerating such behavior from others, it's important to set boundaries and prioritize relationships with those who uplift and support us.

9. **Tolerance of injustices:** It's important to stand up for what is right and just, even when it may be uncomfortable or inconvenient. Tolerating injustices around us only perpetuates them and prevents progress toward a more equitable society.

10. **Tolerance of self-doubt:** Doubting ourselves and our abilities can hold us back from pursuing opportunities and achieving personal growth. While it's natural to experience

self-doubt at times, we must not let it control us or prevent us from taking risks and reaching our goals.

11. **Tolerance of fear:** Fear can also hold us back from pursuing opportunities for growth in both our personal and professional lives. Learning to push past fears and take calculated risks is essential for personal development.

12. **Tolerance of excuses:** Making excuses for ourselves or others only hinders progress toward personal growth and success. Holding ourselves accountable for our actions is crucial for achieving our goals.

13. **Tolerance of Indiscipline:** Lack of discipline can result in a lack of consistency and stability in one's life. Not having a plan for what you need to do each day can make it more likely that you'll put things off and forget to do important things. This can make you disorganized and less productive. Taking steps towards establishing a routine and committing to a set of values or goals can greatly improve the quality of one's life. It makes you unproductive and procrastinate. It is crucial to overcome indiscipline in both personal and professional life and focus on accomplishing goals efficiently.

14. **Tolerance of false beliefs:** Would you agree if I say that you live in lies more than in reality? But this is the truth. This is the reason why many people suffer and very few enjoy life. Holding onto untrue beliefs and living without questioning them won't lead to success. If you challenge your beliefs and open yourself up to learning the truth, it could significantly benefit you in many ways.

15. **Tolerance of judgment:** What if I say, you are lazy or useless or something bad about you? Would you agree? Mostly No, right? Relying on the opinions of others about ourselves and conforming to them will only result in us becoming unproductive instead of achieving greatness. It's foolish to trust the opinions of individuals who make hasty judgments without careful consideration. It's important to keep in mind that the number of people who judge is higher than the number of people who take action. Your life can become incredibly beautiful once you grasp this concept and rid yourself of the tendency to tolerate judgment from others.

16. **Tolerance to criticism:** Have you ever been in a position where you allowed people to criticize you? Have you reacted to them or ignored them? Did they stop criticizing you from the time? I hope your answer is no. This is the problem here. The more you let others criticize you, the more you become vulnerable to their attacks. Their presence can make you feel like you've been plunged into the depths of hell. You are constantly being mocked and treated like a clown. This really hurts. You need to stop tolerating such criticism.

From the above list, we will discuss a few important types of tolerances we should stop growing in us. We will dive deeper and understand how they are harmful and how to unlearn them. We will go through some examples and stories to understand better. Let's dive into the next section.

Wisdom Snippet #5

"Let go of the safety net of tolerance and dare to challenge yourself; you'll be amazed at how far you can soar."

A. Stop tolerating mediocrity

I magine you believed in your dream so strongly. People said that you can achieve it. You also believed you could do it. You worked hard on your dream, and you succeeded in the process. You feel proud of yourself. People praised you a lot for your success. Won't this make you happy? Of course yes.

Now imagine you didn't believe in your idea. Even people told you that you couldn't achieve it. You gave up on your dream believing yourself and others words. Someone else became very successful with the same idea. But you didn't even try. Will it make you happy? No, right?

In the first instance, you believed you could do it, and you know you deserve it, and ultimately you succeeded in achieving your goal. You didn't tolerate mediocrity and gave up on your goal. In the second instance, it's quite the opposite. You tolerated mediocrity and gave up on your goal, which gave you pain.

Let me tell you this secret about great people. Some people, like scientists, artists, entrepreneurs, and leaders, were told they don't have what it takes to succeed and were discouraged from chasing their dreams. Do you think they agree upon that? No.

This is why we know them as great. They didn't accept they were less or incapable. Instead, they worked hard to prove others wrong and also to achieve what they really deserve in life.

The great didn't tolerate mediocrity. They didn't settle for anything less than they deserve. They challenged people's beliefs about them. They proved they are capable. They made a huge difference by allowing them to be free from mediocrity.

Now imagine what you can do with this simple yet powerful rule in life.

You were taught the opposite most of the time. You were told to live the reality instead of dreaming big. You were told not to forget your position. You were always discouraged to live an average life even though you deserve better. You were taught to tolerate mediocrity to live a happy life. If you don't get what you deserve in life, how can you be happy?

You can see how mediocrity affects your life and realize that society teaches you what is easy and comfortable, to put you in control. It's time to get out of this tolerance to mediocrity. Take an oath that you will never settle for something less than you deserve.

Pursue your dream no matter what

We have recognized the adverse impact of accepting mediocrity. You must be determined to aim for the best and not settle for anything less than that. Stop giving in to the negative thoughts within yourself and the negative opinions coming from others. You deserve to surround yourself with positive influences and thoughts that empower you.

Believe in your capabilities and never give up on your dreams. Take steps towards improving your self-esteem and devise a concrete strategy for realizing your aspirations. Many successful people have proven that this truly works, as evidenced by their life stories.

Story time:

This is a true story. A teenager wants to become a doctor. His desire is so strong. But he has two problems: 1. His parents are middle class and can't afford good college 2. His parents and family told him to quit his goal, and it's too big for him.

He believed these two things to be true, and he quit his goal by taking a degree. Then he did his masters. Then he started to work. He gets paid enough that meets his needs. But his desire always haunted him. He is never happy. He didn't know what his life's purpose was. He. He didn't hate his work, and also he didn't love it too.

The time passed, and his dead desire kept haunting him and turned his life into a regret. You may say, he has to move on. But the truth is it's hard to move on. We understand this when we are in other shoes.

Now he has money, and he can afford, but he has no time. He already lost his valuable years just believing and tolerating his situation. This made him give up his goal. Like him, there are many people in this world who lost their dreams, but those dreams keep haunting them.

Personal check:

Ask yourself these questions:

    1. What was your goal when you were a kid?

2. Why did you choose it as your goal?

3. Did you pursue it? If not, why?

4. Are you really happy without pursuing your goal?

5. Are you happy with your present career?

Answering these questions helps you identify missed opportunities and accomplishments. You will also know whether your dreams you killed are haunting you or not. The most important thing you will realize is what you tolerated and how it affected you and your goal.

Solution:

You need to remember the following things and never forget them:

- Do not allow negativity, neither from yourself nor from others, to influence you.

- Ask for advice from someone who has good experience but never live in it because you are not the same as them. If someone is speaking without any experience, then mostly ignore such advice.

- Don't tolerate family, friends and society if they are not supporting your dream. Ignore them until you succeed.

- Make a solid plan and follow it in small steps every day.

- Learn from your failures and do better next time.

- Don't allow people around you to tell you what you have to achieve. You decide what you really want in life. Even if you fail, it's alright, because you will have the satisfaction of trying.

- Always remember there will be alternate methods. Don't just give up tolerating your situations. Take time but pursue what you really love.

Don't accept anything less than what you really deserve (JOB/CAREER)

Many people accept less than they deserve, which is unfortunate. Life is brief, so if you accept less in your daily routine, you will never achieve fulfillment. You should strive for more instead of allowing feelings of hate and irritation to consume you for not taking action.

Having a poor mindset is a curse, not a blessing. It's important to turn down gifts that are not worthy of you and only accept what you truly deserve. Doing so can bring about a profound shift in your entire outlook on life, including your concept of success.

Many people serve as living proof of this. Perhaps you have also settled for less due to some reason. Living a life that you don't truly desire can leave you with a sense of regret, which comes from this form of tolerance.

Story time:

I am surprised to find this out from an HR. One day, I had a chat with one of my friends, who is an HR at a top company. She told me something really important which I teach to others. When people attend for the interview, they say yes to everything, which is completely wrong. They say YES because they want that job. They decrease their value to fit the job and I feel this is wrong.

If you lose yourself for a job, you become nothing and your tolerance has no value. If you stand strong until you get what is fit for you. It's completely different. Even when packages are 2 to 10 lakhs, people say okay for 2 lakhs instead of negotiating for 10 lakhs which is the maximum limit. This looks so foolish.

When you had a change to go for more, why would you settle for less? This is all because of fear of losing that job that makes you live a hell. I am not supporting this kind of mindset. Such a mindset will never give you great results, not a great life. What's the point of this poor mindset?

Tolerating less out of fear without even trying is a great menace. I would not advise anyone to do this. But this is what happens in real time every day. Many teenagers and youngsters agree upon this poor mindset which is not good.

Personal check:

1. Have you attended any interviews?

2. What are the rules and regulations? Did you agree to them if you didn't like them?

3. How much salary is offered to you? Are you happy with it? Or did you ask for more?

Answering these questions gives you a clear idea of what you tolerated that made you unsuccessful. If you realized it now, at least don't repeat the mistake. Always go for more and never tolerate less than what you truly deserve.

Solution:

Follow these rules from the next time:

- Always be ready for any career completely.

- Develop your skills so you feel better for any job.

- Always expect more and try to achieve it.

- When anything is offered, see if it really fits. If not, leave it.

- Never settle for less pay when there is an opportunity to get more.

- Always research your career market well to see the scope and pay accurately.

That's it. I discussed two important sections in this for people who want to pursue a goal or who want to be in a great job because you are going to live with them for a very long time. So these two are very important. Let's dive into the next section which is about yourself completely.

Wisdom Snippet #6

"Never settle for less than you deserve, for the world will only give you what you demand."

B. Stop tolerating INDISCIPLINE

This term is familiar to all of us. I am speaking about indiscipline. Throughout our lives, we have an underlying expectation that others should abide by certain standards. The lack of discipline is not limited to a particular age group or location, such as school or college. It applies everywhere if you observe carefully.

Indiscipline is when people disregard rules and behave in an uncontrolled manner. This is the true meaning of indiscipline. We all disregard rules and regulations which help us in our growth because of comfort or laziness. This results in our failures.

All your failures and negative mindset are the result of your lack of discipline. If you tolerate indiscipline every day, it results in a poor lifestyle which you will hate. Indiscipline can lead to myriad consequences. In essence, I can declare that due to your lack of discipline, both you and those around you will ultimately find your life to be meaningless.

Imagine yourself waking up every day early in the morning with a purpose. You are very productive that you achieve your every work on time without fail. You make progress at every step. You get attention and respect from others. Would all these make you happy? Most of you would say yes.

A disciplined lifestyle can make all of these possibilities a reality. Isn't it amazing? We tolerate indiscipline because our bodies seek comfort. Comfort is the enemy of growth and discipline. Even though we know the effects of indiscipline, we accept it only because of our addiction to comfort. This kind of tolerance will inhibit your growth to a great extent.

The effects of discipline are as follows:

- Lack of interest to try out things

- Postponing your work every time

- No interest in taking risks

- Compromising with your goals or desires

- Small thinking and poor lifestyle

- Becoming physically and mentally inactive.

- Losing interest in everything and everyone

There are numerous effects, which can vary depending on each individual's lifestyle. Not being disciplined can cause long-term problems that may be hard to fix, especially if you lack discipline for a while.

You must stop tolerating indiscipline to live this short yet beautiful life to the fullest.

Story time:

I have a friend who is undisciplined in his life. He is rich which is inherited, but he is mentally poor. He indulged himself in spending money and time each day, experiencing pleasure. He lost all his money because of his bad way of living.

He overslept daily. He did no job. He spent money on his friends and parties. He lived a life without a purpose. He lived it for a mere joy. Now he suffers every day with poverty. His friends left him. He got no proper job.

This is all because of the indiscipline he had developed within him. Indiscipline results in every loss. I am speaking about the personal discipline that should be developed which helps in our growth. If he has developed a proper discipline in his life. He would have not ended up like this.

He agreed that he tolerated indiscipline, which put him in such a position. Once he realized this he began a small business by borrowing a loan, and now he has made a proper life that is disciplined and successful.

Personal check:

Now ask yourself these questions:

- Have you ever been undisciplined in your life?

- Did indiscipline give you good results?

- Is there anything you quit or gave up because of poor mind-set?

- Have you ever checked the effects of indiscipline?

- Have you ever postponed your work and suffered?

- Write everything you felt with indiscipline in your life.

Answering these questions gives you a clear idea of what indiscipline does to you. Indiscipline is something which prevents you from taking risks, trying new things, accepting change and there are many more adverse effects. So I hope you understand why you should stop tolerating indiscipline in your life.

Solution:

Once you find out how indiscipline is effecting you, it's time to take action. There are several ways that work for beating indiscipline. But the simple one is to stop thinking and start acting small now.

You know we all dwell in our thoughts and comfort instead of working on what we really want in life and this is a bad habit that we all grew in us which suppresses our growth. Not taking care of this will lead to indiscipline which affects you in the long term.

Follow this simple method to beat indiscipline:

This method is simple yet effective in the long term.

1. Get up from your comfort place.

2. Stop thinking so much.

3. Make a simple plan of what you want to achieve and in what time. (Don't forget to do a reality check on your plan)

4. Work in small steps on your plan.

5. Check progress and improve where necessary. (Note: Maintain a small notebook and a pen to record everything.)

6. Reflect, learn and improve from your results. That's it. (Always improve your plan if necessary and stick to it)

7. Maintain proper timing for everything.

This method can be applied to learn and unlearn habits that build or destroy your discipline.

Pro check:

Numerous exceptional leaders, companies, and organizations refuse to tolerate anything that hinders their growth. The main reason why they stand strong and become examples for others is their discipline. As an individual, you can truly distinguish yourself from the crowd and achieve greatness by refusing to tolerate indiscipline in your life.

Wisdom Snippet #7

"Tolerance for indiscipline only perpetuates chaos and hinders progress; it's time to reclaim our power by setting higher standards."

C. Stop tolerating toxic relationships

Harmful relationships can be toxic and ultimately disturb mental well-being, leaving one in a state of unrest. Many people stay in toxic relationships because they are afraid of being alone and have become dependent on their partner.

Many people hold onto harmful relationships without realizing the long-term consequences. At some point, everyone has to realize that being alone is better than being in a toxic relationship.

Once you acknowledge the detrimental effects of toxic relationships on your life, you will attain genuine freedom and awareness of your actions. You will comprehend how tolerating such relationships is affecting you.

Imagine you brought a small plant that produces your favorite fruit. You want to grow it well so that you enjoy the delicious fruits of it. But instead of pouring water every day if you pour a drop of poison on it. What do you think will happen?

You got it, absolutely correct. It will die soon. It doesn't matter how much you try to bring it to life. Once dead, you cannot grow it back normally. A toxic relationship can have a harmful impact on our lives, much like a plant being slowly killed by a small amount of poison each day.

Even small amounts of toxic behavior in our everyday relationships can devastate our emotional well-being. In order to eliminate toxicity in a relationship, both parties must be willing to make an effort toward the resolution. If not, it will be unproductive and negatively affect your mental well-being, leading to mental decline.

This analogy effectively demonstrates the harmful impact of toxic relationships on our lives. Toxic relationships cause pain and problems in life, despite your efforts. It is preferable to remain alone rather than be in a relationship that deprives you of your happiness and peace.

Story time:

I know someone who agreed to marry a girl chosen by his parents without knowing anything about her. After getting married, he discovered that she was unfaithful and had feelings for someone else.

She only agreed to the marriage because of her parents. When confronted, she apologized and promised not to repeat her mistake. However, she was lazy and never kept her promises. She didn't value her husband's words and only did what was comfortable for her.

At first, he was hopeful and intelligent, but he soon became lazy and hopeless like her. She was his other half, so he ended up becoming like her since she didn't change. This is what a toxic relationship looks like. He gave up on his dreams and desires and his lifestyle became worse.

All of this happened because he tolerated a toxic relationship. In my opinion, if a relationship is not helping you grow, it's better to end it than to be stuck and rot away.

Personal check:

Check if your relationship is toxic by reviewing these points.

- Is your relationship inhibiting your growth?

- Is it giving you more sadness?

- Are you constantly discouraged by your partner?

- Is your partner controlling or trying to control every aspect of your life?

- Are you feeling alone even though you are with your partner?

- Do you trust each other very much?

- Are you constantly stressed out?

- Are you anxious all the time?

If you answered yes to these questions, it is likely that you are in a toxic relationship. Read on to find out what to do with your toxic relationship.

Solution:

1. **Communicate:** Effective communication plays a crucial role in fostering strong and healthy relationships. The more effectively you communicate, the greater the likelihood of resolving a toxic relationship. It is crucial to openly share all aspects of your thoughts and emotions with your partner, even the smallest desires, fears, and dislikes. Furthermore, it is important to express the things you wish for your partner to improve upon.

2. **Understand:** Understanding your partner's aspirations and mindset is crucial. Every relationship carries more weight than just adding another person to your life. It means embracing their aspirations, values, behaviors, and perspectives as well. It is essential to show respect to all individuals as long as they are genuine and contribute positively to personal development.

3. **Work on improvement together:** Stop cultivating negative habits that hinder personal and relationship growth. You should start working together to improve. Get rid of the habits that cause you to lose hope and feel uninspired. If you or your partner lack great aspirations, it is important to at least offer them support or seek support from them.

4. **Grow Trust:** Trust is the foundation of any successful relationship. Trust is essential in every relationship. Trust is the foundation of any relationship; without it, success is impossible. Always be truthful, do your best, share everything, and never lie, no matter what the outcome may be. Your lies will cause people to lose trust in you. Be honest and don't pretend.

5. **Work for mutual growth:** Know what you want from each other to grow. If any partner fails, growth becomes impossible. So share what's wrong and fix your mistakes and don't repeat it. Support each other's aspirations and help each other at every step. Always give hope to your partner to try and live their goals. Never discourage them if they fail while pursuing their dreams.

If a relationship fails to bring happiness, then it's time to step away and find happiness elsewhere. Don't fear being alone. Being alone is preferable to being a lifeless corpse.

Wisdom Snippet #8

"We tolerate a lot because we don't want to lose people. But what you forgot is tolerance makes you lose yourself."

D. Stop tolerating false beliefs

Consider the scenario where someone deceives or betrays you. How would you react to such an occurrence? Would you experience positive emotions or negative ones? It is safe to assume that the majority of individuals would feel a sense of discomfort and develop a strong dislike towards the person responsible for their deception or lies. This reaction is perfectly normal and can be observed even in mundane situations we encounter in our daily lives.

Have you ever considered the implications of someone deceiving you about the way you should live and understand life? This includes the rules you ought to adhere to for personal growth, relationship guidance, career advice, and even starting your own business.

False beliefs that have no impact on our personal development may be tolerable, but the ones that are ingrained in us and constrain our mindset are truly detrimental. I am speaking about such beliefs which you should stop tolerating.

The hardest and sad part is breaking these beliefs that are learned by us and taught by society which create poor mindsets. These beliefs come from systems and people who want to control us and be our rulers.

Story time:

Many students work hard and effectively. I know lots of students who don't work. If I tell these students, you are not worthy, and you will fail in life. Do you think all these students will fail to live their lives?

Opinions may vary, with some saying yes and others saying no. Allow me to disclose the reality. I have come across numerous individuals who have secured a prosperous life solely through their intelligence, without putting in much hard work or studying. To be honest, despite their lack of academic success, they managed to surpass the hardworking individuals in their careers. The education system provides the knowledge and skills necessary to succeed in a chosen profession. But this is not true for many.

The educational system produces a workforce but often neglects to nurture brilliant minds. The life stories of many great people teach this concept. Think of all the great men and women you are familiar with. If you go through their stories, you'll grasp the reality. However, society teaches that education is crucial for success, but it is a misconception.

Personal check:

Let's verify if this statement is true.

Has anyone ever encouraged you to aim high and put in the effort to achieve your goals?

Did your school encourage you to work hard to create a lifestyle that benefits others or only to find a job?

Are careers like doctor, engineer, manager only important? (What about actors, artists, great writers?)

Do you feel like taking no risks and have a comfortable, secure life?

Do you think a job is better than your own business empire?

Have you given up your passion or goal by accepting the reality or your current situation?

Answering these questions will give you clarity on why you should stop tolerating false beliefs in life. The rules and beliefs are created to put us in control and to create evenness in the society, but life doesn't work like that. The society is taming you and turning you into domestic social animal who is scared of taking risks.

Remember that we are all born wild. We love risks. We love challenges. Society teaches us to conform and suppress our potential, hindering us from developing a growth mindset. When you realize this one thing and act, you will become an ultimate beast who will take risks and never miss any opportunity.

Follow these steps to change your false beliefs and become truly free and untamed.

Solution:

To stop tolerating false beliefs, here are some steps you can take:

1. **Recognize your own biases:** Biases can affect how we evaluate beliefs. Try to take a moment to step back and analyze if there are any preconceived notions or biases that might be affecting your willingness to embrace false beliefs.

2. **Seek reliable sources of information:** Search for trustworthy sources of information that offer evidence-supported

information. Never believe what people say or information that you found from other sources. Always check whether the information you receive is genuine or not. Only after a check, rely on information to create your real belief systems.

3. **Engage in critical thinking:** Improve critical thinking to assess beliefs. Pose questions, question presumptions, and thoroughly analyze the evidence supporting the assertions being presented.

4. **Foster an open mind:** Develop a mindset that is open and receptive to different viewpoints and perspectives. This does not imply embracing every belief, but rather being open to new information and evidence. Always welcome new ideas and filter them by checking whether they are true or not.

5. **Surround yourself with diverse perspectives:** Expanding your perspective by surrounding yourself with individuals who hold a diverse range of viewpoints can greatly enrich your understanding and debunk any misconceptions.

6. **Fact-check regularly:** Always make sure to verify the correctness of information before accepting it as fact or disseminating it to others. Verifying the accuracy of claims can be achieved by using fact-checking websites or seeking advice from experts in the field.

7. **Be mindful of cognitive biases:** Familiarize yourself with different cognitive biases that might have an impact on your way of thinking and decision-making, including confirmation bias or availability bias. Knowing these biases can stop you from being caught in their traps.

Remember that changing long-held beliefs takes time and effort, so be patient with yourself throughout this process.

Wisdom Snippet #9

"True progress is impossible without the courage to dismantle the foundation of false beliefs."

E. Stop tolerating Negative influences

Do you know about weeds? What happens if you don't remove them from the crop? They compete with useful crops, taking away sunlight, nutrients, water, and space. Just like that, negative people take advantage of your resources and hinder your personal growth, having the same detrimental effect on those around them.

This only happens when you allow negative people to influence you. By tolerating them, you are the one giving them the opportunity to take advantage of you. Negative people can be a problem, but it's worse when you let their negativity control you and make you less effective. It is wiser to avoid any negative influence in your life. It benefits both your mental well-being and your personal development.

Your poor mindset and lifestyle are a direct result of the negative influences in your life. They are the ones manipulating you to fulfill their own desires.

Story time:

A fox lived in a dark forest. It was clever. It cleverly used its intelligence to find food each day. The trap caught many animals, and they became its food.

Once upon a time, a fire erupted in a certain area of the forest. To escape from the fire, all the birds took flight from the trees. The tortoise wanted to escape but couldn't because it couldn't fly.

The fox was hungry and safe, far from the fire. The tortoise was seen and chosen as a meal. It began to cheer on the tortoise, shouting for it to leap out of the fire.

The tortoise was scared and confused about the situation. The tortoise followed the fox's advice and tried to fly over the fire. But it used too much energy and fell into the fire, getting burned.

The fire stopped due to the rain and the fox ate the dead tortoise. The tortoise's life was lost due to its own foolishness and the fox's influence.

MORAL: Never come under the bad influence. Such influence always brings pain and suffering in life.

This story can convey the message why you should never come under negative tolerance in life. Remember to avoid bad influences, no matter the situation. Negative influences have no concern for your well-being; they are solely focused on themselves.

Personal check:

Are people you spend time with helping you in growth or stagnation?

Do you have a strong mindset?) What is the prevailing mindset of the people around you or your friends?)

It's true that the mindset of the people you surround yourself with can significantly influence your own mindset.

Do you always prefer being lazy and staying in your comfort zone?

Are you someone who enjoys taking risks or do you prefer to stay on the safe side?

Analyzing and answering these questions can provide you with a clearer understanding of yourself. This helps you determine if you are influenced by negativity. Now that you have discovered it, it's time to put a stop to tolerating these negative influences that hinder your personal development.

Solution:

To stop tolerating negative influences, consider the following steps:

1. **Identify the negative influences:** Pause and reflect on the people, situations, or actions that could negatively affect your overall well-being and mental state.

2. **Set boundaries:** Set clear boundaries to shield yourself from these negative influences. You may need to limit interactions with certain people or avoid certain places.

3. **Surround yourself with positivity:** Surround yourself with individuals who exude positivity and encouragement, lifting your spirits and filling you with motivation. Engage in activities that promote positivity and personal growth.

4. **Practice self-care:** It is essential to prioritize your physical, mental, and emotional well-being. Be mindful of your needs and participate in activities that foster self-care and enhance your overall well-being.

5. **Develop a positive mindset:** Nurture a positive outlook by regularly engaging in gratitude exercises, visualizing your success, and reinforcing positivity with affirmations. Challenge negative thoughts and replace them with positive ones.

Keep in mind that liberating yourself from negative influences requires time and dedication, yet it can ultimately bring about a more rewarding and optimistic existence.

Wisdom Snippet #10

"In a world filled with darkness, be the beacon of light that refuses to let negativity overshadow your brilliance."

F. Stop tolerating injustice

Picture a situation in which a student is a witness to the daily bullying endured by their classmate at school. The student is aware that this behavior is unfair and unacceptable, yet they decide to endure it by staying silent and taking no action to support their classmate. By allowing this unfairness, the student not only continues the bullying but also adds to the victim's pain, causing lasting emotional and psychological harm.

Tolerating injustice lets it continue and hurt people. We need to take action against injustice to make a fairer and kinder society.

Imagine you are a hardworking employee who has put in countless hours and effort into your job. You consistently meet deadlines, exceed expectations, and contribute to the success of your company. However, despite your dedication, you notice that your colleague gets promoted ahead of you, not because of their skills or accomplishments, but simply because they have a personal connection with the boss.

In this scenario, tolerating this injustice for yourself would mean accepting that your hard work and talent will never be recognized or rewarded fairly. By staying silent and allowing this unfair promotion to go unchallenged, you are perpetuating a system that values nepotism over meritocracy.

By tolerating this injustice for yourself, you not only undermine your own self-worth and limit your career growth but also send a message to others that it is acceptable for favoritism to trump hard work. This creates a toxic work environment where employees become demoralized and disengaged, impacting overall productivity and success.

Instead of tolerating such injustice, it is essential to speak up and advocate for fairness. By raising awareness about the issue and seeking support from colleagues who may share similar experiences or values, you can create momentum for change. This could involve discussing the situation with HR or higher management, presenting evidence of your qualifications, or even pursuing legal action if necessary.

By refusing to tolerate injustice for yourself and taking action against it, not only do you give yourself a chance at receiving the recognition you deserve but also contribute towards creating a more equitable

I believe that the two examples mentioned above are quite fundamental, yet powerful, and are sufficient to illustrate the profound impact of tolerating injustice. It is not only harmful to tolerate injustice when it is done to oneself but also when one witnesses others suffering due to someone's wrongdoing and chooses to remain silent.

The examples I previously provided are also applicable in real time. I have witnessed many unfair situations, questioned them, and faced consequences for them. However, I feel proud of myself because I stood up for what was right.

Story time:

I'll share two stories that show how tolerating injustice can cause harm.

1 I have a friend who is employed as an accountant in a company. As soon as he began his job, his superior treated him exceptionally well. However, as time went by, my friend's diligent efforts and rapid learning became a source of jealousy for his senior. Consequently, the senior started relentlessly blaming and complaining about my friend to the boss every single day. This significantly reduced his opportunities for salary increases and career advancement. My friend knows this very well, but he didn't stand up for himself. He stayed silent and tolerated injustice.

This led to a sense of desperation and a complete lack of interest in his work, causing him to gradually lose motivation and become increasingly unproductive. This situation will ultimately have a negative impact on both him and the company. You may say the mistakes are the fault of the senior and the boss who blindly accepted what was said. I agree with their opinions, but my friend, who is the real issue, should learn to defend himself.

2 At a certain school, a teacher noticed that some students were receiving preferential treatment and more attention than others simply because their mother was a staff member. Allowing them to neglect their work and education is a foolish decision. The main objective of attending school is to acquire knowledge and skills. If one fails to achieve this, then attending becomes pointless, and time and money are wasted.

However, some of the students faced disciplinary action and were subjected to unfair treatment. The school teacher's fair treatment of every student ignited the anger of a mother on the staff. To take vengeance, she fabricated stories about the teacher, who had disciplined her children for neglecting their responsibilities.

The teacher persisted and reported the truth to the school management, resulting in the mother being terminated from staff, which was the appropriate action. This made the learning environment equal for all students and the ones who received special treatment improved their learning. This is the result of standing up against unfairness. By reading these two stories, you will gain a better understanding of why it is important to refuse to tolerate injustice.

Standing up against injustice may cause you to lose some people and even gain some enemies, but the benefits are invaluable as it empowers both yourself and others, and brings a sense of true happiness and contentment.

Personal check:

Do you work harder than others but feel unappreciated?

How do you feel when you see individuals who are less skilled than you, but are promoted successfully simply because they know how to please your boss?

Do you come across biases and choose to remain silent in school, workplace, or society?

Would you embrace schemes or rules that pose a threat to you and society?

Would you condone the unethical behavior and dishonesty of poor leaders?

Answer these questions and discover if you can truly experience genuine happiness. Transform yourself and refuse to tolerate any injustice, anywhere.

Solution:

To stop tolerating injustice, here are some steps you can take:

1. Educate yourself: Begin by gaining knowledge about the multiple types of injustice that exist within society. This includes understanding systemic oppression, discrimination, and inequality. Read books, watch documentaries, follow reputable news sources, and engage in discussions to gain a deeper understanding.

2. Speak up: You must not remain quiet in the face of injustice, whether you witness it or experience it. Speak out against discrimination and lend your support to those who are marginalized. Let your voice be a catalyst for change. Spread awareness by having meaningful conversations with friends, family, and coworkers both in-person and on social media platforms.

3. Challenge your own biases: Reflect on your own beliefs and biases that may contribute to tolerating injustice. Engage in self-examination to uncover any unconscious prejudices or assumptions you may hold. Be open to correcting these biases through education and personal growth.

4. Support organizations dedicated to justice: Contribute to organizations working towards justice and equality by volunteering your time or donating money if possible. Research local grassroots initiatives or national/international organizations that align with your values and lend them support.

5. Allyship: Stand in solidarity with those impacted by injustice by becoming an ally. This involves actively supporting marginalized communities while recognizing their unique experiences and amplifying their voices without overpowering them.

6. Practice empathy: Try to understand other people's experiences without judging or invalidating them. Imagine how injustice impacts their daily lives if you put yourself in their place. Help them in all possible ways.

7. Promote inclusivity: Actively work towards creating inclusive environments where everyone feels heard, valued, and supported regardless of their race, gender identity, sexual orientation, religion, disability status, or any other factor that makes them unique.

8. Vote responsibly: It is crucial to take part in all levels of elections - be it local, regional or national - to vote for leaders who give priority to justice issues and work towards implementing policies that support equality for everyone.

9. Report incidents of injustice: If you come across instances of injustice or discrimination, make sure to report them in the right way. This may include informing the authorities, human rights organizations, or other relevant entities who can take immediate action to resolve the issue.

10. Join advocacy groups: Join local or national advocacy groups that fight against injustice. Working together with people who share your values and beliefs can lead to the creation of a fairer and more equal society.

Remember, fighting against injustice is an ongoing commitment. It requires continuous learning, self-reflection, and taking action whenever possible. Start small but be persistent in your efforts to make a positive change in the world.

Wisdom Snippet #11

"Today's injustice will become tomorrow's regret if we do not take a stand and rewrite history with compassion and equality."

G. Stop tolerating excuses/failures

Most people fail because they make excuses instead of pushing themselves harder and striving for success. They embrace failures and endure the consequences that come with them. Allowing excuses and accepting failure will not lead to productive outcomes.

This rule is known by many great and successful individuals. They never search for excuses or speak about their failures. They work harder. They are solely interested in seeing outcomes, not hearing excuses or witnessing failures. They are highly successful because they don't tolerate excuses or failures.

They learn from their mistakes. They rectify their mistakes and gain the wisdom to steer themselves towards the path of success.

To achieve remarkable success, adopting a mindset that shuns excuses and failures is imperative. Your top priority should be reaching your goal and satisfying your innermost aspirations. When you experience this, success will follow shortly after.

Story time:

My neighbor has a Master's degree in business administration. He always dreamed of landing a position at a prestigious company. Although his desire is strong, his mental strength may not be at the same level.

He is not good at communicating. He enrolled in several courses with the aim of enhancing his communication skills. He also went to several interviews. He couldn't communicate well, so most people didn't accept him. He stopped trying and started making excuses like "Job hunting is hard" or "Interviews are difficult."

After struggling for some time, he came to the realization that his aspirations were beyond his capabilities. Therefore, he acknowledged that he was not deserving of achieving his ultimate objective. This incident drained his hope and forced him to accept excuses and failure.

Rather than learning from his failures, he chose to surrender to despair. This situation has caused him to become an average person. He was unhappy and confused. He failed to get back on track because he found excuses to justify his lack of progress. He had a strong belief that he was a failure.

After a few years of not working, he began operating a small fruit stand. Though it earned him a meager sum, he remained unhappy as he was unable to fulfill his deepest desires.

This is simply because he allowed excuses to comfort himself and embraced failures without extracting lessons and developing through them.

This is why you should not tolerate excuses. This is why you should not tolerate failures. You must put an end to making excuses and begin moving forward. Confronting failures and learning from them is crucial, as the lessons they teach us become the blueprint to success. It's important not to forget these valuable lessons.

Personal check:

Do you have any deep desire that you gave up?

Are you happy with your current career?

Have you tried your idea more than 100 times?

Do you think failures are good?

Do you often complain about everything?

Do you blame others for your problems or mistakes?

By answering these questions, you will gain clarity on whether you are accepting excuses and failures in your life or not. If you have indeed discovered that, then it is imperative to cease such behavior as this habit negatively impacts your personal development.

Solution:

Stopping the tolerance of excuses or failures requires adopting a proactive mindset and implementing effective strategies. Here are some steps to consider:

1. Take ownership: Accept responsibility for your actions and outcomes. Recognize that making excuses or accepting failure without taking action will hinder personal growth and progress.

2. Set clear goals: Clearly define your goals and establish specific actions needed to achieve them. This clarity helps you stay focused and motivated, reducing the tendency to make excuses or tolerate failure.

3. Analyze past patterns: Think back to times when you may have made excuses or allowed failure to be acceptable. Identify the underlying causes, such as fear of failure, lack of confidence, or poor time management. Understanding these patterns empowers you to address them effectively.

4. Develop resilience: Embrace a resilient mentality by viewing setbacks as learning experiences rather than failures. Learn from mistakes, adjust your approach, and keep moving forward with determination.

5. Create an action plan: Break down your goals into smaller, manageable tasks with deadlines. Creating a structured plan not only provides a roadmap for success but also minimizes the room for excuses.

6. Hold yourself accountable: In order to stay committed to your goals, it's important to establish systems of accountability. You can simplify this by setting weekly goals, tracking your progress in a journal, or talking to a trusted friend or mentor for support and guidance.

7. Challenge limiting beliefs: Identify any self-limiting beliefs that contribute to making excuses or tolerating failure. Replace negative thoughts with positive affirmations that reinforce your capabilities and potential for success.

8. Surround yourself with positivity: Surround yourself with people who inspire and motivate you towards excellence. Seek out mentors, coaches, or like-minded individuals who share similar values and encourage personal growth.

9. Practice self-discipline: Cultivate self-discipline by following through on commitments regardless of circumstances or challenges that may arise along the way. This builds character and reinforces a mindset focused on action rather than excuses.

10. Celebrate progress: Acknowledge and celebrate even the smallest achievements along the way. This helps foster a positive mindset and encourages continuous effort towards your goals, reducing the temptation to use excuses or tolerate failure.

Remember, stopping the tolerance of excuses or failures is an ongoing process that requires self-reflection, commitment, and consistent effort. Stay persistent, stay accountable, and keep pushing yourself to reach new heights.

Wisdom Snippet #12

"Excuses may temporarily soothe the ego, but they will never heal the wounds caused by failure."

H. Stop tolerating criticism

Imagine you allowed someone to criticize you. You ignored them and walked away without responding. Do you think they will not criticize you next time?

They will keep criticizing you. They will mistreat you constantly. Some of you may have experienced receiving criticism from someone at some point in your life. Try to remember it. Have you ever faced a situation where you didn't let people criticize you?

It's possible that people you know have created satirical works about you and mocked you in front of others. In the long run, this not only diminishes the respect others have for you, but also erodes your own self-respect.

Criticism can greatly affect our self-confidence and diminish our charm if we don't work to stop tolerating it.

If someone criticizes you again, assertively express that you aren't willing to put up with it. Make it clear that you won't tolerate it. Some individuals may cease their criticisms towards you while others may persist, but eventually even they will put an end to it. Don't give up. Remind them that you don't like being criticized.

If someone receives criticism while learning or working on a project or passion, they may feel discouraged and may not want to continue. Allowing criticism from others as well as accepting that criticism and living with it will affect your life.

You have two choices: either reject criticism or let others criticize you without being affected.

When examining the stories of successful individuals, it becomes clear that they faced criticism at some point or another. Consider the multitude of individuals, including entrepreneurs, artists, visionaries, scientists, and countless others who have achieved incredible success in their lives. They faced criticism, but they kept going and achieved their goals, impacting their own lives and the lives of others.

Story time:

Imagine a scenario where you have been working tirelessly on a project, pouring your heart and soul into every detail. Excited to share your hard work with others, you present your creation to a group of peers, hoping for praise and encouragement. Instead, what follows is an onslaught of criticism - everything from the color scheme to the font choice is torn apart.

Now, ask yourself: Is tolerating this kind of criticism truly beneficial? Does it motivate you to improve or does it leave you feeling demoralized and disheartened? The answer is clear.

Let's take a stand against tolerating unwarranted criticism. By refusing to accept baseless negativity, we can foster an environment where constructive feedback thrives. Just like in the world of design or any creative endeavor, constructive feedback fuels growth and improvement.

Imagine if Steve Jobs had succumbed to the naysayers when he first introduced the iPhone – "It's too expensive," "Who needs a touchscreen?" -he would have missed out on revolutionizing the way we communicate today. Similarly, J.K. Rowling faced countless rejections before Harry Potter became a global phenomenon. Had she given up in the face of debilitating criticism, her incredible storytelling would have remained hidden from millions.

By taking a stand against tolerating criticism without merit, we empower ourselves and those around us to rise above negativity and strive for greatness. It's time to shift our focus towards constructive feedback that helps us grow instead of allowing baseless criticism to hold us back.

One more story which proves this concept:

Two foxes lived in a forest. The lake near the village is a popular spot for them to take a break and quench their thirst. Naughty kids would also go there to play. Whenever they spotted a fox, they would taunt it by hurling stones, causing the fox to flee in fear.

It happened daily, and the children made the fox suffer daily. The fox always ran away.

Another fox took the place of the old fox that used to run away from the mischievous kid. The children always threw rocks and bothered it. The fox didn't run away. Instead, it started to pounce on them and hunted them until they all ran in fear.

What do you understand from this story?

While the first fox accepted the mistreatment from the children and endured the pain, the second fox refused to tolerate such behavior. This scared the kids, and they never bothered the foxes again.

We should all stop tolerating criticism. By doing this, we will not only benefit ourselves but also assist others.

Personal check:

Did you accept criticism from others?

Have you witnessed individuals experiencing distress due to criticism?

Have you ever abandoned your aspirations because others have criticized your ambitious dreams?

Does it bring you joy when people criticize you?

Have you ever faced those who have criticized you?

Answering these questions will help you understand how tolerating criticism has affected you. You will also see why it is important to stop tolerating it in order to earn respect from others and yourself.

Solution:

To stop tolerating criticism, it's important to develop a strong sense of self-worth and cultivate emotional resilience. Here are some steps you can take:

1. Recognize your own value: Don't let others' opinions or criticisms determine your worth as an individual. Stay focused on your strengths, achievements, and the positive aspects of your life.

2. Change your point of view: Instead of considering criticism as an offense to you or a proof of your incompetence, attempt to regard it as a chance to develop and enhance yourself. Embrace constructive feedback as a chance to learn and develop yourself further.

3. Understand the intention behind the criticism: Consider the motives behind the critic's remarks. Are they genuinely trying to help you improve, or are they being unnecessarily negative or hurtful? By understanding their intentions, you can better assess whether their criticism is worth taking seriously.

4. Evaluate the validity of the criticism: Assess whether the criticism has any merit by objectively examining the content and reasoning provided. If there is truth in what is being said, use it constructively to make necessary changes in areas where you see fit.

5. Practice self-compassion: Be kind to yourself when faced with criticism. Remember that everyone makes mistakes and has room for growth. Treat yourself with compassion rather than harsh judgment, allowing room for improvement without beating yourself up.

6. Surround yourself with positive influences: Surrounding yourself with a circle of people who support and uplift you, and who value and inspire you, can greatly boost your self-confidence and provide you with a more holistic perspective when facing criticism.

7. Develop coping mechanisms: Explore strategies like deep breathing exercises, meditation, or journaling to help manage any negative emotions that arise from criticism. These techniques can help you maintain calmness and clarity while responding constructively.

8. Use assertive communication: Instead of taking criticism personally or getting defensive, develop assertive communication abilities to calmly and directly express your emotions while establishing clear boundaries about the type of feedback that is beneficial for you.

9. Reflect on your achievements: Regularly reflect on your accomplishments, skills, and successes to build self-confidence. By acknowledging your worth and capabilities, it will become easier to brush off unfounded or unconstructive criticism.

10. Set realistic expectations: Accept that criticism is a natural part of life. Nobody is completely immune to it. Understanding this can help you develop a more balanced perspective and let go of the need for perfection.

Remember, not all criticisms are valid or constructive. Learning how to discern between genuine feedback and baseless negativity can help you minimize the impact of undeserving criticism on your well-being.

Wisdom Snippet #13

"When you stop tolerating criticism, you create space for authentic self-expression and unleash your true potential."

I. Stop tolerating judgment

D o you recognize the cage we inhabit? It's intriguing how it remains unlocked, yet many hesitate to step out. This is about the cage of others' opinions and our fear to defy them. This cage becomes stronger through our fragile mindset. Transforming a negative mindset into a positive one removes limitations and reveals opportunities.

Regrettably, most of us are too scared of personal transformation to try this change. When we concern ourselves with others' judgments, we accept their view as our reality, hindering our growth and potential.

Therefore, stop worrying about what others think or say about you. Their opinions don't define us - remember that. We should stay authentic and not let external views restrict us or undermine our potentiality. Embrace being unique; follow your own life path without fear.

Story time:

Two students were branded as failures by their teacher. Both of them initially accepted this harsh judgment.

One student internalized the teacher's words, believing he was indeed useless and incapable of success. As an adult, his life reflected these beliefs; he struggled with menial jobs to support himself and his family.

The other student chose to defy the teacher's assessment. He worked diligently on self-improvement, identifying his strengths in physical tasks rather than memorization - a skill highly valued in school. This realization inspired him to enhance his physical abilities while also elevating his memory from being below average to an average level. His confidence soared even higher than those deemed 'toppers'.

His newfound self-belief landed him a prestigious job where ironically, the so-called 'toppers' worked under him. He started his own company and hired people with above-average memory skills, achieving great success by rejecting the negative judgment passed onto him.

This story illustrates how life can dramatically shift when you reject others' judgments and believe in yourself instead. Working on what you genuinely love changes your perception about life and makes it more meaningful.

Personal check:

Have you ever tolerated judgement?

Does tolerating judgement make you happy?

Have you limited yourself because of judgement from others?

Do you care about what others think about your lifestyle?

Are you living your own life or the life dictated by others?

Answering these questions will help you understand the effects of tolerating judgement and why you should stop tolerating it.

Solution:

To stop tolerating judgment, here are a few steps you can take:

1. Recognize your self-worth: Remind yourself that judgments from others do not define you. Build your self-esteem and confidence by focusing on your own strengths and achievements.

2. Challenge your beliefs about judgment: Question the validity of the judgments you receive. Consider whether they come from reliable sources and whether they align with your values and goals.

3. Develop empathy: Understand that everyone has their own perceptions and biases. Put yourself in the shoes of the person judging you, and try to understand their point of view without taking it personally.

4. Surround yourself with supportive people: Surrounding yourself with positive, non-judgmental individuals can help counteract any negative effects of judgment. Seek out friends and loved ones who uplift you and accept you for who you are.

5. Shift your mindset: Instead of viewing judgment as an attack or criticism, reframe it as an opportunity for growth. Use constructive feedback to improve yourself rather than allowing it to bring you down.

6. Practice self-compassion: Treat yourself with kindness and understanding when faced with judgment. Remember that nobody is perfect, including yourself, and that making mistakes is a part of learning and growing.

7. Set boundaries: Be clear about what kind of behavior is unacceptable to you. Communicate your boundaries assertively but respectfully when dealing with judgmental individuals.

8. Focus on personal growth: Instead of dwelling on external judgments, channel your energy into personal development and pursuing your goals. By focusing on self-improvement, external opinions become less relevant.

9. Detach from the need for approval: Shift your focus from seeking validation from others to finding fulfillment within yourself. Cultivate a strong sense of self-approval based on your own values and aspirations.

Remember that dismantling the pattern of tolerating judgment takes time and effort. Be patient with yourself as you work towards creating a healthier mindset and surrounding yourself with positivity.

Wisdom Snippet #14

"Free yourself from the burden of constantly seeking approval and watch how liberating life becomes."

J. Stop tolerating fears

Fears can have a negative impact on our lives by limiting our mental development and preventing us from seizing opportunities. They can hold us back from reaching our full potential and experiencing new things. They induce lethargy, diminish hope, and lead to a life of regret.

People often give in to their fears instead of facing them, which can lead to a boring and unsatisfying life. The fear of failure is the most common reason why individuals settle for a compromised life. The fear of taking risks and the fear of criticism hold us back.

It's important to understand that fear not only stifles progress, but also hinders us from reaching our ultimate goals. When you understand that you need to overcome obstacles and take risks to achieve your true desires, you will be ready to face any challenge. This determination will elevate you to greatness, making you a source of inspiration for others.

Story time:

There is a young student named Sarah who dreams of becoming a doctor. She excels in her science classes and has a natural curiosity for the human body. However, Sarah's fear of failure and rejection constantly holds her back from pursuing her aspirations.

Sarah tolerates this fear by convincing herself that she is not smart enough or capable enough to achieve her dreams. Instead of taking the necessary steps towards medical school, she settles for a less challenging career path that offers minimal personal growth.

Sarah's fears prevent her from reaching her full potential and also stop society from benefiting from her passion and talent in medicine. If we continue to tolerate these fears within ourselves, we risk losing countless innovators, leaders, and visionaries who could contribute greatly to our world.

It is time to stop tolerating fears like Sarah's. We must challenge ourselves to overcome these limitations and pursue our passions with unwavering determination. Only then can we unlock our true potential and make meaningful contributions that shape our future for the better.

Personal check:

Are your fears limiting you?

What are the fears that are limiting you?

What fears do you think have prevented you from pursuing your fears?

Have you faced your fears or gave up because of fears?

Have you seen fears or are they illusions?

Have you taken risks?

Answer these questions and analyze them. Understanding the impact of our fears is crucial to breaking free from their hold and achieving true happiness through the pursuit of our dreams. It's time to stop allowing these fears to hold us back and start living the life we truly want.

Solution:

I've faced these fears myself. I made wrong decisions out of fear and preferred comfort over risk-taking, which stifled my abilities. I felt lost until I realized that fear is merely an illusion we create in our minds—most often learned from society.

So, I decided to confront my fears with a simple plan: list them down on paper. My biggest fear was public speaking. To overcome this, I began reading about it and started practicing by joining clubs or speaking at small institutions. Initially terrifying, but as I continued speaking publicly, the fear lessened and replaced by excitement.

Overcoming your deepest fears requires action—doing what scares you most—a lesson learned late in life but deeply valuable nonetheless.

Next up was overcoming my second-biggest fear: solo travel combined with acrophobia (fear of heights). So, I began traveling alone to places situated at great heights, initially closeby then further away each time enjoying the view more than fearing it.

The key takeaway? Repeatedly facing your fears not only eradicates them but also makes those activities enjoyable, boosting confidence and happiness levels significantly.

This method helped me face my fears and feel freer, which is an important step towards living life fully.

Remember: don't let your fears limit or destroy your one precious life! Face them head-on take risks, enjoy the journey along the way, live life to its fullest potential.

Tips to work effectively on your fears:

1. Identify your fears: Take time to acknowledge and understand what specific fears you are tolerating in your life. This can include fear of failure, rejection, uncertainty, or any other type of fear.

2. Acknowledge the impact: Recognize how these fears are affecting your life, happiness, and overall well-being. Understanding the negative impact they have can motivate you to overcome them.

3. Challenge your thoughts: Many fears are based on irrational beliefs or exaggerated scenarios. Question the validity of these thoughts and challenge them with rational thinking. Ask yourself if there is evidence to support your fear or if it's just a perception.

4. Take small steps: Break down your fears into manageable tasks and take small steps towards facing them. Start with less intimidating situations and gradually expose yourself to more challenging ones. This gradual exposure will help build confidence and reduce fear over time.

5. Seek support: Don't hesitate to reach out to friends, family, or professionals for guidance and support in overcoming your fears. Sharing your concerns with others can provide different perspectives and valuable advice.

6. Learn relaxation techniques: Fear can bring about anxiety and stress, making it harder to confront and overcome our fears. Practice relaxation techniques such as deep breathing exercises, meditation, or yoga to calm your mind and reduce anxiety levels.

7. Focus on positive outcomes: Instead of focusing on the negatives of facing your fears, imagine the positive results and concentrate on the benefits of overcoming them. Stay motivated by reminding yourself of the personal growth and opportunities awaiting you beyond fear.

8. Celebrate progress: Acknowledge every small step or achievement towards overcoming your fears. Recognizing progress will reinforce positive behavior and encourage further growth.

9. Embrace failure as learning: Understand that failure is an essential part of growth and development. Accept that setbacks may occur along the way but view them as opportunities for learning and improvement rather than reasons to give up.

10. Practice self-compassion: Be kind to yourself throughout the process. Overcoming deep-rooted fears takes time and effort, so be patient with yourself and celebrate your courage and resilience along the way.

Remember, overcoming fears is a gradual process. It requires consistent effort, patience, and self-compassion. With each step you take, you'll become more empowered to live a life free from the limitations of fear.

Wisdom Snippet #15

"Courage isn't the absence of fear, but rather the decision to no longer let it dictate your choices."

PART 6

Preventing Recurrence of Tolerance habit

Congratulations on successfully understanding the concept of stop tolerance. Well done! You have reached your highest level of personal growth and have a determined mindset to only accept the best in all areas of your life. You care about progress, not excuses. You care about your dreams, not fears. Don't hold back and strive for success every single time.

Learning new and good habits is time-consuming but falling back to your old bad habits is very fast. This habit of tolerating things that has been limiting you until now may occur again. So, I request you to be careful so that you don't get back to your old habits of tolerance.

In this section, we will deal with some ways and tips that will help you with preventing this recurrence.

Let's get started.

I will be sharing some habits that can assist you in developing a mindset which will stop the tolerance habit from resurfacing. Continue reading.

A. Learn to say NO

Mastering the art of saying No is absolutely essential in life. If you constantly struggle to say No, you are allowing yourself to be undermined by accepting things that diminish your worth in life.

Reject anything that causes you discomfort and doesn't contribute positively to your personal development. You might find yourself in an unsatisfactory job, a toxic romantic relationship, or a detrimental friendship. Anything that hinders your progress, joy and inner harmony. Say No to all of them.

Saying no can empower you to take control of your own time and priorities.

For instance, imagine a scenario where a colleague asks you to stay late at work to help them with a project that they should have completed themselves. By saying no and setting boundaries, you are asserting your worth and ensuring that your own tasks and personal life are not compromised. This refusal communicates self-respect and encourages others to take responsibility for their own actions, ultimately fostering a more balanced and productive work environment.

It's important to say No to many things in life. The only filter you have to use is whether saying no is beneficial for you or not. Also, consider if it contributes to your well-being and personal growth. It's important to evaluate the impact of saying no on your own priorities and goals.

Saying No is like engaging in a battle with your own mind. If you've broken your habit of stopping tolerance once, you can start it again. Don't feel bad or guilty.

Refusing to accept tolerance is strongly connected to mastering the ability to say No. Zero tolerance is all about saying No to many things that inhibit your growth. This means the same thing as having no tolerance for something.

Saying no to others can be quite inconvenient. However, it is beneficial that you engage in this activity for your own well-being. You are preventing people from avoiding using you whenever they have their own needs.

Here are some tips to help you say "no" to people politely and assertively:

1. Be clear and direct: Clearly state your answer without any ambiguity. This helps prevent misunderstandings or confusion.

2. Use "I" statements: Expressing your decision from a personal perspective can help the other person understand that this is your choice and not a reflection on them.

3. Offer alternative solutions: If appropriate, suggest alternatives or compromises that might work for both parties involved.

4. Practice active listening: Show empathy and understanding towards the other person's request, but make it clear that you cannot fulfill it.

5. Stay firm and confident: Avoid wavering in your response or apologizing excessively. Remember, it's okay to prioritize your needs and boundaries.

6. Be respectful: Use polite language and maintain a respectful tone throughout the conversation, even if the other person becomes pushy or insistent.

7. Don't over-explain yourself: You don't need to give a long list of reasons or excuses for saying "no." Keep it simple and concise.

8. Thank them for understanding: If the person accepts your rejection gracefully, express gratitude for their understanding.

9. Practice saying "no": Role-playing or rehearsing with a friend can help you feel more comfortable and prepared when faced with saying "no" in real-life situations.

10. Take care of yourself: Remember that setting boundaries is essential for your well-being. Saying "no" when necessary allows you to prioritize what matters most to you.

Wisdom Snippet #16

"No is a complete sentence, and sometimes the most powerful one you can use."

B. Develop a growth mindset

Having a growth mindset is crucial for achieving greatness and making significant contributions. It all boils down to how you manage your mistakes and failures, and your ability to handle pressure and stress in life.

The more effectively you handle negativity, stress, and unavoidable pressures, the stronger you will become mentally. This will greatly contribute to developing a growth mindset. Learn from mistakes and failures to improve.

The growth mindset enables you to maintain the habit of not giving up for a longer period of time, or even indefinitely. Appreciate this way of thinking.

Here's one of my favorite analogies:

The artist began sculpting a stone into a beautiful artwork. The stone was too painful for him to carve, so the artist couldn't carve it because it became hard. The artist skillfully carved another stone that turned into a precious work of art, enduring pain and pressure. In contrast, the first stone was ignored and rendered useless.

In life, we all experience pressures as we grow up and we must accept them. To cultivate these habits of not tolerating things, it is crucial to embrace the challenges and hardships that come along the way. By viewing them as opportunities for personal development, you pave the path towards achieving success.

Have the persistence to continually search for methods to enhance yourself and become an even greater individual. Always believe in yourself and have this growth mindset.

If you want to develop a growth mindset, here are some tips to consider:

1. Embrace challenges by seeing them as opportunities to grow and expand your abilities. It can help you learn new skills too.

2. Cultivate a positive attitude by focusing on the potential for learning and improvement in every situation. Even when setbacks happen, see them as temporary and try to find ways around them.

3. Stay curious and open-minded to new learning experiences. Try to explore different ideas, perspectives, and approaches to develop your skills further.

4. Practice resilience by learning to bounce back from failures. Use your mistakes and setbacks as stepping stones towards progress rather than allowing them to discourage you.

5. Establish goals that are within reach. Make them specific and realistic to your abilities. Divide them into smaller steps or milestones to monitor your progress effectively.

6. Acknowledge the importance of effort and persistence: Acknowledge that making an effort is necessary for personal development and

improvement. Focus on consistently putting in hard work and avoid relying solely on inherited talent or abilities.

7. Encourage feedback from others to learn and grow without taking it personally.

8. Emphasize the learning process: Instead of focusing solely on the end result, pay attention to the learning process itself. Celebrate incremental progress along the way, rather than only valuing the final outcome.

9. Surround yourself with positive influences: Surround yourself with people who support and inspire you towards personal growth. Engage in activities or join groups that nurture a culture of growth mindset.

10. Practice patience with yourself: Remember that developing a growth mindset takes time and effort. Be patient with yourself during the process, and celebrate every step you take forward, no matter how small it may seem.

By following these tips, you can develop a mindset that values growth and reach your full potential for success, personal development, and learning.

Wisdom Snippet #17

"Success is not determined by how far you've come, but by how much you've grown along the way."

C. Set Boundaries

Everyone dislikes having restrictions placed on them. It is human nature to prefer freedom and autonomy. Imposing limitations can feel constricting and frustrating for individuals. Thus, it is understandable that nobody likes limits.

This entire book emphasizes the importance of living beyond limits, specifically outside of one's comfort zone. However, it is necessary to establish boundaries or limits for ourselves in order for growth to occur.

Here are 5 simple tips to help you set boundaries and prevent tolerance that hinders your personal growth:

1. Understand your values: Take time to reflect on your core values and priorities in life. This will help you identify what is important to you and what you want to prioritize in terms of personal growth.

2. Define your limits: Determine what behaviors, situations, or actions are not aligned with your values or hinder your personal growth. Clearly define those limits for yourself so that you can communicate them effectively when needed.

3. Communicate assertively: Practice expressing your needs, desires, and boundaries in a clear and respectful manner. Use "I" statements to communicate how certain behaviors or actions affect you personally.

4. Say no when necessary: Learn to say no without feeling guilty or obligated. Be selective about the commitments, tasks, or requests you take on. Prioritize your own well-being and growth by assessing whether something aligns with your goals and values before agreeing to it.

5. Surround yourself with supportive people: Surround yourself with individuals who uplift and encourage your personal growth journey rather than those who enable toleration of behaviors that hold you back. Seek out friends, mentors, or support groups that promote self-improvement and hold you accountable for establishing healthy boundaries.

Remember, setting boundaries is an ongoing process that requires practice and self-reflection. By taking small steps towards establishing healthy boundaries, you can create an environment that fosters personal growth and fulfillment in all areas of life.

Wisdom Snippet #18

"Boundaries are like road signs, guiding us towards healthier relationships and protecting our emotional well-being."

D. Overcome obstacles and failures

No matter what you begin, there will always be obstacles. Success is obtained when you are able to overcome these obstacles. When you encounter these obstacles and cannot overcome them, it results in failures.

You always need to overcome these obstacles and failures to prevent desperateness while trying to fulfill something or while learning something.

When you're trying to stop being tolerant, you'll face many obstacles that can be painful. Sometimes you may feel like giving up and end up failing. But don't worry, you can always get back on track from the beginning. Don't let fear of failure make you lose hope. Never lose hope; instead, believe that you will conquer obstacles and achieve success.

To overcome obstacles and failures while learning to break the tolerance habit for personal growth, consider the following tips:

1. Embrace a growth mindset: View obstacles and failures as opportunities for learning and improvement rather than setbacks or indications of your abilities.

2. Analyze and learn from failures: Take the time to analyze what went wrong and identify any patterns or areas for improvement. Use failure as a stepping stone towards personal growth.

3. Seek support and guidance: Don't hesitate to reach out to mentors, coaches, or supportive friends who can provide guidance, advice, and perspective during challenging times.

4. Adopt resilience and perseverance: Develop resilience by staying positive, maintaining a sense of determination, and adapting to new circumstances. Persevere through challenges with focus on your long-term goals.

5. Practice self-compassion: Treat yourself kindly when you encounter failures or setbacks by practicing self-compassion. Remember that no one is perfect, and everyone experiences ups and downs on their personal growth journey.

6. Set achievable goals: Break down your larger goals into smaller, manageable tasks that can be accomplished gradually. This approach will help build momentum and prevent overwhelm in the face of challenges.

7. Celebrate small victories: Acknowledge and celebrate even the smallest achievements along the way to reaffirm your progress and stay motivated during difficult times.

8. Cultivate a supportive environment: Surround yourself with people who uplift you, encourage your growth, and understand that setbacks are part of the learning process. Avoid negative influences that perpetuate self-doubt or hinder your progress.

9. Practice self-reflection: Regularly take time to reflect on your experiences, successes, failures, insights gained, lessons learned, and areas in need of further growth. Use this reflection to adjust your approach moving forward.

10. Stay committed to personal growth: Dedicate yourself to continuous learning, improvement, and evolution – even when faced with obstacles or failures. Remember that personal growth is a lifelong journey, and each experience holds an opportunity for transformation.

By following these tips, you can overcome challenges, grow personally, and reach your full potential.

Wisdom Snippet #19

"A setback is merely a set-up for an even greater comeback; let your determination soar higher than any obstacle."

E. Stay focused and be patient

It's important to always keep in mind that maintaining focus and being patient are essential when it comes to achieving anything. If you lack focus and patience, you will not accomplish anything remarkable. To ensure success, it is vital to remain focused and avoid any setbacks while adopting this new habit.

In order to maintain focus and patience, it is essential to remain resilient and fully engaged in order to achieve desired outcomes.

The majority of individuals struggle with multitasking, which is why I advocate for concentrating on one task at a time until you successfully accomplish it. Concentrate on overcoming one specific habit of tolerance at a time. Although it may take time, this approach will enable you to enhance your focus and witness undeniable results.

Imagine you are a gardener, tending to a beautiful rose bush. You've put in countless hours of hard work, from planting the seedling to carefully nurturing it with water and nutrients. Now, all that remains is for the buds to bloom into gorgeous, vibrant flowers. It's easy to feel a rush of excitement and impatience as you eagerly wait for those first blooms.

If you're impatient and start digging up the soil too soon or constantly disturb the plant, you might harm its fragile roots. Allow the roses to grow naturally and be patient while providing the care they need.

In doing so, you witness the miraculous transformation unfold before your eyes as each bud slowly opens up into an exquisite blossom. The reward for your patience is not just one or two flowers, but an entire garden filled with radiant colors and intoxicating fragrance.

Similarly, in our daily lives, we often face situations where staying focused and being patient can yield remarkable results. Whether it's working towards professional goals or nurturing relationships, rushing or becoming easily distracted can hinder progress. By remaining steadfast in our efforts and embracing patience, we allow ourselves to fully appreciate the blossoming outcomes that come with time.

So let us remember this humble rose gardener's example - stay focused on our aspirations and be patient along the way. Just like those breathtaking roses, success will eventually flourish before us if we nurture it diligently and trust.

One more way is to create a contingency plan. Create a plan for what you want to achieve.

- Consider what you want to achieve.

- Divide the plan into smaller, manageable steps that can be accomplished each day.

- Dedicate time to each step and accomplish it promptly.

- Focusing on your goal and refusing to tolerate anything that hinders your progress should be your utmost priority.

- Keep track of your advancements.

- Take a moment to evaluate your progress and determine what adjustments should be made.

- Take the opportunity to glean valuable lessons from your failures, ensuring you rectify any errors in future endeavors.

- Continue persevering until you attain the outcomes you aspire for.

Having a plan allows you to maintain focus and avoid getting sidetracked.

To stay focused and be patient, consider the following tips:

1. Set clear goals: Define what you want to achieve and break them down into smaller, actionable steps. Having specific goals will help you stay focused and motivated.

2. Prioritize your tasks: Identify the most important tasks that align with your goals and tackle them first. Avoid getting overwhelmed by focusing on one task at a time.

3. Create a conducive environment: Minimize distractions by creating a dedicated workspace that is free from noise and interruptions. Turn off notifications on your phone or computer to maintain focus.

4. Practice mindfulness: Cultivate mindfulness by being fully present in the moment. Train yourself to refocus whenever your mind starts wandering or gets distracted.

5. Use productivity techniques: Experiment with different productivity techniques, such as the Pomodoro Technique or time blocking, to help you stay focused for specific periods of time.

6. Take breaks strategically: Breaks are essential for maintaining focus and preventing burnout. Schedule short breaks between tasks to recharge and rejuvenate your mind.

7. Practice patience: Recognize that personal growth takes time and effort. Stay committed to your process and avoid getting discouraged if results don't come immediately.

8. Reflect on progress: Regularly reflect on how far you've come by keeping track of your achievements and lessons learned along the way. This can boost motivation and reinforce patience.

9. Seek support when needed: Surround yourself with supportive individuals who can offer guidance, encouragement, and accountability during challenging times.

10. Celebrate small wins: Acknowledge and celebrate each milestone achieved along the way, no matter how small it may seem. This helps maintain motivation and boosts confidence in your progress.

Remember, staying focused and being patient is a continual practice that requires effort and self-discipline. Be kind to yourself during this process, allow for setbacks, but keep moving forward towards personal growth.

Wisdom Snippet #20

"In a world of constant distractions, staying focused is not just a skill but a superpower that unlocks limitless possibilities."

F. Be Self-compassionate

To foster self-compassion and promote personal growth, it's essential to cease tolerance of behaviors or situations that hinder your progress. Recognize the importance of being kind and understanding towards yourself, allowing for mistakes and setbacks without judgment. By engaging in self-compassion, you can overcome obstacles and pave the way for personal development.

Self-compassion is the practice of being kind to yourself and offering help and support to your own well-being, just as you would do for others. It involves extending the same understanding, care, and empathy to yourself that you would show to someone else in need. Never compromise what helps you grow.

When you face difficulties and try to make changes, it's normal to feel like giving up. However, if you give yourself support and keep moving forward, you will become the best version of yourself. Always remember this while learning anything useful for your growth.

Here are 5 unique and simple tips to be more self-compassionate and let go of tolerance that hinders your growth:

1. Embrace imperfections: Accept that making mistakes is part of being human. Instead of criticizing yourself, choose to learn from your failures and celebrate your progress.

2. Set healthy boundaries: Learn to say "no" when needed. Prioritize your needs and well-being by setting clear boundaries with others. This will prevent you from tolerating situations that hold you back.

3. Practice self-compassion: Treat yourself with kindness and understanding, just as you would a dear friend. Speak to yourself in gentle and supportive language, offering comfort during challenging times.

4. Release expectations: Let go of the pressure to always be perfect or meet unrealistic standards. Accepting yourself as you are, without judgment or comparison, allows for personal growth and freedom from self-inflicted limitations.

5. Foster a growth mindset: View challenges as opportunities for learning and growth rather than obstacles to overcome. Embrace new experiences, seek feedback, and believe in your ability to improve over time.

Remember that self-compassion is a journey that requires patience and practice. To truly unlock your full potential and cultivate a genuinely compassionate mindset, it's essential to incorporate these valuable tips into your daily routine. By doing so, you will overcome any obstacles that stand in your way.

Wisdom Snippet #21

"In the pursuit of self-improvement, don't forget to be gentle with yourself along the way - progress takes time and self-compassion."

Conclusion

In life, you have the power to take control of your own path or surrender that power to others. It all comes down to what you can accept in life. If you tolerate something that helps you grow, it's good tolerance. But if you tolerate something that hinders your growth, it's bad tolerance and you should stop tolerating it.

People tolerate wrong things in the modern world. They tolerate many things that disturb their mental peace and happiness, which results in them becoming absolute failures. This book is a lifesaver for anyone who is enduring hardships in life and feeling down. Especially for people who are being affected by the habit of tolerance.

When you learn to reject anything that prevents your personal growth, you will unlock your full potential to achieve amazing things without needing to compromise. Going through stop tolerance habit helps you become who you truly are. It helps you stop becoming a people pleaser. Most important of all, it turns you into a human who cares and does what is right every time.

Remember that not every tolerance is good for our growth. Some tolerances help us grow, and some tolerances inhibit our growth. When you know the difference, you make a difference.

You will also transform into a more authentic, disciplined, and respectful individual, who is compassionate towards themselves and acts with righteousness in every aspect.

Caution:

If your aim is to be self-sufficient and formidable without sacrificing your way of life, then this is the book for you. If you want to make others happy, this book may not be suitable for you because it suggests separating from anyone who prevents your progress. If you prioritize being around the wrong kind of people over your personal growth, then this book may not be suitable for you.

To truly foster personal growth and independence, one must be willing to release any negative influences. Therefore, I highly suggest reading this book only if you are ready and willing to let go of anything inhibiting your progress. This book is specifically designed for individuals who have a strong sense of self-love and a deep desire for ultimate and remarkable personal growth.

This book is intended for individuals who take action rather than those who only have aspirations. This book is intended for individuals seeking to develop their character and attitude positively.

Welcome aboard if you agree to abide by the aforementioned rules.

About the Author

Manikanta Belde

Manikanta Belde is a multi-talented writer who excels in a wide range of genres. The author has written various works that encompass a wide range of genres. These genres include motivational tales, brief fictions, manuals for personal improvement, and character-building materials. He is also a personal development blogger, Digital Content creator and founder of Manikanta Belde Inc, Blink Talks, and The Life School.

He is motivated by a strong desire for personal growth and business ventures. His goal is to encourage people to enhance their lives and tap into their full abilities to attain success.

He writes and creates content in English. He has been living in Hyderabad for 7 years.

Learn more about Manikanta Beldi at:

https://www.amazon.com/author/manikantabelde

http://manikantabelde.com/

manikantabelde@gmail.com

Follow him on Instagram at:

https://www.instagram.com/manikantabelde/